W9-BXV-543

Indulgence

Indulgence

MURDOCH
BOOKS

CONTENTS

LIVE TO EAT

Lord Byron's declaration in his epic poem *Don Juan* that 'Since Eve ate apples, much depends on dinner', is something to consider next time you're planning a special meal. One of the first—and most important—steps in a successful seduction is a memorable dinner. It doesn't matter whether you're entertaining friends or cooking just for two, a menu that's been well planned and prepared can set the seal on any relationship. These are recipes for people who want to live well, love well and eat well.

GLOSSARY

As our interest in different cultures expands, so does our knowledge of more exotic cuisines. Good food demands great produce: using top-quality ingredients will ensure maximum flavour and texture in the meals that you serve. Whatever their country of origin, most of these items are now readily available either at the supermarket or in greengrocers or delicatessens. Buy the best you can afford and taste the results.

ASIAN GREENS (FROM LEFT TO RIGHT)

Chinese broccoli is also known as gai larn. It has slightly leathery leaves and thick, green stems—both are used in cooking. *Bok choy* (pak choi) is a mild vegetable related to Chinese cabbage. It is great stir-fried, braised or steamed and needs very little cooking. *Choy sum* is otherwise known as flowering cabbage and often has yellow flowers. The stems and leaves are eaten.

BIRD'S-EYE CHILLI

A very hot, small red or green chilli about 1–3 cm (1/2–1 in) long. They can be bought fresh, dried or pickled in brine, but fresh is best.

COUSCOUS

This is a granular semolina. A favourite in North African cuisine, use it as a base for other flavours. Couscous is best steamed so it turns out light and fluffy. Instant couscous, the most common variety, cooks very quickly.

EXTRA VIRGIN OLIVE OIL

Essentially the same as virgin olive oil, but with very low acidity, it comes from the first pressing of olives. It is not really suitable for cooking as the flavour is lost when heated but it is great with pasta or in salad dressings. Extra virgin olive oils vary in flavour according to where they come from. Taste a few until you find one that you really like.

FISH SAUCE

This seasoning is popular in South-east Asian cuisine. Made by extracting the liquid from salted, fermented fish, it is a clear brown liquid with a pungent salty flavour. Use it sparingly as the flavour is very strong.

KAFFIR LIME LEAVES

The leaves from the kaffir lime tree (also known as makrut), are dark green and aromatic with an incomparable flavour and perfume. They are available fresh, frozen or dried—the fresh leaves have an especially intense flavour. Each leaf in made of two pieces joined by one central vein. In our recipes, we have treated one half of the figure of eight as one leaf.

LEMON GRASS

A thick-stemmed herb with pale green-grey leaves, lemon grass has a lemony flavour and aroma and is an important ingredient in Thai cuisine. The thicker, paler part of the stem is most commonly used. Dried lemon grass is available but it has an inferior flavour. Peel the tough outer layers of the stem off until you reach the first purple-tinged layer.

MUSHROOMS (CLOCKWISE FROM LEFT)

Oyster mushrooms are fan-shaped and pale creamy grey or brown with a mild peppery flavour. *Shiitake mushrooms*, originally from Japan and Korea, are aromatic and meaty and are available either fresh or dried. The stems are tough and must be discarded, but can be used in stock. *Shimeji* are a delicate-tasting Japanese mushroom grown in clumps. They have a slightly concave cap on a long stem. *Enoki* have very long stems and tiny caps. They have a yeasty or fruity flavour and can be eaten raw or cooked.

11

PALM SUGAR

Palm sugar, or jaggery, is popular in South-east Asian foods. It is an unrefined sugar sold in blocks or jars and ranges in colour from pale gold to dark brown. It is a richly flavoured, aromatic sugar extracted from the sap of various palm trees. Soft brown sugar can be substituted. The easiest way to get palm sugar off a block is to grate it.

POLENTA

These coarsely or finely ground dried grains of corn are used in savoury and sweet dishes. Polenta (also known as cornmeal) can be served either soft or firm, depending on the coarseness of the grain and the amount of liquid used. Instant polenta takes only a few minutes to cook.

PRESERVED LEMONS

Lemons are preserved in salt for about 30 days and develop a soft texture and a distinctive, pungent flavour. They are popular in Moroccan cookery, but should be used sparingly. Rinse well and remove the white pith and flesh before using.

PUY LENTILS

A small, slate green pulse from France. Reputed to have the best flavour and texture of all lentils, they hold their shape when cooked. Buy them in gourmet food stores or delicatessens. They are eaten as a side dish or as a base for savoury meals.

RED ASIAN SHALLOTS

Small purplish-red onions with a concentrated flavour, commonly used in Asian cookery. They grow in bulbs and are sold in segments that look like large cloves of garlic. If necessary, you can substitute one small red onion for 3–4 red Asian shallot segments.

SAFFRON THREADS

These reddish-orange threads are the stigmas of the crocus flower. Saffron is the most expensive spice in the world, but only a small amount is needed to give a vivid colour and a subtle flavour. The strands are generally infused in a little hot liquid before using.

SEA SALT FLAKES

These flakes come from the evaporation of sea water. Sea salt flakes have a clean flavour that's perfect for the table or in cooking.

VANILLA BEAN

A long, thin pod that is the fruit of a large orchid. Highly aromatic, it has a rich, smooth flavour that is often infused into desserts. The seeds from the pod can also be scraped into liquid for extra flavour and to give a speckled appearance.

STARTERS
& SOUPS

After a long hard week, there's nothing more enjoyable than sitting down in your own home to the kind of food you'd normally go out for. Whether you're cooking a special meal at home just for two, or entertaining on a more lavish scale, it's the first course that sets the scene for your dinner party. Just as a good breakfast kick-starts your day, so too can a delicious and tempting starter get your guests in the right frame of mind.

CORN AND LEMON GRASS SOUP
WITH YABBIES

SERVES 4 (6 AS A STARTER)

This spicy soup is based around the deliciously moist meat of the yabby—a freshwater crayfish found in dams, rivers and lakes and available from your fish market, unless you can catch your own.

Preparation time: 30 minutes
Total cooking time: 1 hour 50 minutes

4 corncobs
1 tablespoon oil
1 leek (white part only), chopped
1 celery stalk, chopped
3 stalks lemon grass (white part only),
  bruised
5 garlic cloves, crushed
1 teaspoon ground cumin
1 teaspoon ground coriander
3/4 teaspoon ground white pepper
3 kaffir lime leaves
750 ml (3 cups) chicken stock
800 ml (31/4 cups) coconut milk
125 ml (1/2 cup) cream
2 teaspoons butter
1/2 teaspoon sambal oelek
1.2 kg (2 lb 12 oz) cooked yabbies
  or crayfish, peeled and shredded
1 tablespoon finely chopped
  coriander (cilantro) leaves

1 Slice the kernels off the corncobs. Heat the oil in a large saucepan over a medium heat, add the leek, celery and lemon grass and stir for 10 minutes, or until the leek is soft. Add half the garlic, cumin, coriander and a pinch of the pepper and cook, stirring, for 1–2 minutes, or until fragrant. Add the corn, lime leaves, stock and coconut milk, stir well and simmer, stirring occasionally, for 11/2 hours. Remove from the heat and cool slightly.

2 Remove the lemon grass and lime leaves and blend the mixture in batches in a food processor until smooth.

3 Push the mixture through a sieve with a wooden spoon. Repeat.

4 Return to a large clean saucepan, add the cream, and warm gently.

5 Melt the butter in a small frying pan over a medium heat, add the remaining garlic and pepper, the sambal oelek and a pinch of salt and stir for 1 minute. Add the yabby meat, stir for a further minute, or until heated through, then remove from the heat and stir in the fresh coriander.

6 Ladle the soup into shallow soup bowls, then place a mound of yabby meat in the centre of each bowl. Serve.

CAULIFLOWER SOUP WITH SMOKED SALMON CROUTONS

It is best to use day-old bread when making croutons as it won't absorb moisture as easily as fresh bread does. Buy an unsliced loaf and slice it yourself, or ask your baker to do it for you.

Preparation time: 25 minutes
Total cooking time: 35 minutes

CROUTONS

1 loaf day-old white bread, sliced
    lengthways
2 tablespoons butter, melted
1 garlic clove, crushed
150 g (5½ oz) smoked salmon or
    gravlax
1 tablespoon finely chopped dill

SOUP

1 tablespoon oil
1 leek (white part only), chopped
1 garlic clove, chopped
400 g (14 oz) cauliflower, cut into
    florets
1 potato, chopped
250 ml (1 cup) chicken stock
250 ml (1 cup) milk
315 ml (1¼ cups) cream
1 tablespoon horseradish cream
1 tablespoon lemon juice
1 tablespoon snipped chives

1 To make the croutons, preheat the oven to 150°C (300°F/Gas 2). Brush three slices of the bread on both sides with the combined butter and garlic, then season with salt. Cut off the crusts, cut each slice into four long strips, then carefully transfer the strips to a baking tray, spacing them a little apart. Bake for 30 minutes, or until crisp and golden.

2 Meanwhile, heat the oil in a large saucepan, add the leek and extra garlic and cook over a medium heat for 6–8 minutes, or until the leek is soft but not brown. Increase the heat to high, add the cauliflower, potato, stock and milk and bring just to the boil. Reduce the heat and simmer, covered, for 20 minutes, or until the potato and cauliflower have softened.

3 Cool the mixture slightly, then transfer to a blender or food processor and purée until smooth. Return to a clean saucepan and add the cream, horseradish and lemon. Reheat gently for 5 minutes, then add the chives.

4 Cut the salmon into strips the same width as the croutons and lay along the top of each crouton. Sprinkle with the dill. Serve the soup in deep bowls with two long croutons for each person.

SPICED LENTIL SOUP

A staple in many parts of the world, lentils are tasty and versatile. This recipe calls for puy lentils—a slightly smaller variety with a peppery flavour.

Preparation time: 10 minutes + 20 minutes standing
Total cooking time: 50 minutes

1 eggplant (aubergine)
60 ml (1/4 cup) olive oil
1 onion, finely chopped
2 teaspoons brown mustard seeds
2 teaspoons ground cumin
1 teaspoon garam masala
1/4 teaspoon cayenne pepper
   (optional)
2 large carrots, cut into cubes
1 celery stalk, diced
400 g (14 oz) tin tomatoes, crushed
110 g (1 cup) puy lentils
1 litre chicken stock
35 g (1 small handful) roughly
   chopped coriander (cilantro)
   leaves
125 g (1/2 cup) Greek-style plain
   yoghurt

1 Cut the eggplant into cubes, put in a colander, sprinkle with salt and leave for 20 minutes. Rinse well and pat dry with paper towels.

2 Heat the oil in a large saucepan over a medium heat. Add the onion and cook for 5 minutes, or until soft. Add the eggplant, stir to coat in oil and cook for 3 minutes, or until softened.

3 Add all the spices and cook, stirring, for 1 minute, or until fragrant and the mustard seeds begin to pop. Add the carrot and celery and cook for 1 minute. Stir in the tomato, lentils and stock and bring to the boil. Reduce the heat and simmer for 40 minutes, or until the lentils are tender and the liquid is reduced to a thick stew-like soup. Season to taste with salt and cracked black pepper.

4 Stir the coriander into the soup just before serving. Ladle the soup into four warmed bowls and serve with a dollop of the yoghurt on top.

SCALLOPS WITH GOAT'S CHEESE AND CRISPY PROSCIUTTO

SERVES 4 AS A STARTER

It is possible to buy scallops with the coral-coloured roes already removed. Make sure you clean them thoroughly to remove any grit that may remain in the shells.

Preparation time: 10 minutes
Total cooking time: 10 minutes

4 thin slices prosciutto
16 scallops on shells, cleaned and
   roes removed
2–3 tablespoons extra virgin olive oil
1 tablespoon chopped flat-leaf
   (Italian) parsley
100 g (3½ oz) goat's cheese,
   crumbled
2 tablespoons good-quality aged
   balsamic vinegar

1 Cook the prosciutto under a hot grill until crisp, then drain on paper towels and break into small pieces.
2 Put the scallops on two baking trays. Combine the oil and parsley in a small bowl and season with sea salt and cracked black pepper. Brush the scallops with the oil mixture.
3 Cook the scallops in batches under a hot grill for 2–3 minutes, or until they are tender.
4 Top the scallops with the crumbled goat's cheese and prosciutto, then drizzle with balsamic vinegar.
5 Carefully transfer the scallops from the trays to serving plates lined with rock salt—the shells will be very hot.

COCONUT PRAWNS WITH CHILLI DRESSING

Cooked in a variety of fresh spices and coconut cream, this Asian-style dish lets you enjoy good-quality fare with a touch of the exotic at home.

Preparation time: 35 minutes + 30 minutes refrigeration
Total cooking time: 30 minutes

90 g (2 handfuls) chopped coriander
    (cilantro) leaves
24 raw king prawns (shrimps), peeled
    and deveined, with tails left intact
plain (all-purpose) flour, to coat
1 egg
1 tablespoon milk
60 g (1 cup) shredded coconut
2½ tablespoons oil
300 g (10½ oz) red Asian shallots,
    chopped
2 garlic cloves, finely chopped
2 teaspoons finely chopped fresh
    ginger
1 red chilli, seeds and membrane
    removed, thinly sliced
1 teaspoon ground turmeric
250 ml (1 cup) coconut cream
2 kaffir lime leaves, thinly sliced
2 teaspoons lime juice
2 teaspoons palm sugar
3 teaspoons fish sauce
oil, for shallow-frying
150 g (3 handfuls) mixed lettuce
    leaves

1 Set aside 1 tablespoon of coriander leaves. Holding the prawns by their tails, coat them in flour, then dip them into the combined egg and milk and next in the combined coconut and coriander. Refrigerate prawns for 30 minutes.

2 Heat the oil in a saucepan and cook the shallots, garlic, ginger, chilli and turmeric over a medium heat for 3–5 minutes, or until fragrant. Add the cream, lime leaves, lime juice, sugar and fish sauce. Bring to the boil, then reduce the heat and simmer for 2–3 minutes, or until thick. Keep warm.

3 Heat 2 cm (3/4 in) of oil in a frying pan and cook the prawns in batches for 3–5 minutes, or until golden. Drain on paper towels and season with salt.

4 Add the extra coriander to the dressing. Divide the lettuce among four bowls, top with the prawns and drizzle with the dressing.

VEGETARIAN PIZZAS

SERVES 4

A fresh alternative to traditional mozzarella cheese, haloumi is a salty, firm-textured goat's cheese that originates from the Middle East.

Preparation time: 30 minutes
Total cooking time: 50 minutes

6 Roma (plum) tomatoes, halved
   lengthways
60 ml (¼ cup) olive oil
3 whole marinated artichoke
   hearts
50 g (1 handful) basil
2 garlic cloves, crushed
2 tablespoons pine nuts
35 g (⅓ cup) grated Parmesan
   cheese
4 ready-made 17 cm (6½ in)
   pizza bases
175 g (6 oz) haloumi cheese, sliced
   lengthways into twelve thin slices
12 kalamata olives
shredded rocket (arugula), to garnish

1 Preheat the oven to 210°C (415°F/Gas 6–7). Put the tomatoes, cut-side-up, on a baking tray. Drizzle with 1 tablespoon of the oil and season to taste with sea salt and black pepper. Bake for 35 minutes. Remove from the oven, but leave the oven on.

2 Cut the artichoke hearts into quarters, reserving 1 tablespoon of the marinade for later use.

3 To make the pesto, place the basil, garlic, pine nuts and Parmesan in a small food processor or blender and process until roughly chopped. With the motor still running, slowly pour in the remaining olive oil until the mixture becomes a smooth paste.

4 Spread the pesto evenly over each pizza base, leaving a 1 cm (½ in) border. Arrange three tomato halves and three artichoke quarters on each pizza.

5 Pour the reserved marinade over the haloumi, then place three slices of haloumi on each pizza. Top with the olives and bake for 15 minutes, or until the base is crisp. Garnish with the rocket and serve.

CARAMELIZED ONION TARTS
WITH ROCKET AND BLUE CHEESE

SERVES 6

Perfect for a dinner party or to take on a weekend picnic. The sweetness of the caramelized onion complements the full-flavoured blue cheese beautifully.

Preparation time: 30 minutes + 30 minutes refrigeration
Total cooking time: 1 hour 10 minutes

PASTRY
250 g (2 cups) plain (all-purpose)
    flour
125 g (4½ oz) butter, chilled and
    cut into cubes
25 g (¼ cup) finely grated
    Parmesan cheese
1 egg, lightly beaten
¼ cup (60 ml) chilled water

FILLING
2 tablespoons olive oil
3 onions, thinly sliced
2 handfuls rocket
    (arugula) leaves
100 g (3½ oz) blue cheese, lightly
    crumbled
3 eggs, lightly beaten
60 ml (¼ cup) cream
50 g (½ cup) finely grated
    Parmesan cheese
pinch grated nutmeg

1 To make the pastry, sift the flour into a large bowl and add the butter. Rub the butter into the flour with your fingertips until it resembles fine breadcrumbs. Stir in the Parmesan cheese.

2 Make a well in the centre of the dry ingredients, add the egg and water and mix with a flat-bladed knife, using a cutting action, until the mixture comes together in beads.

3 Gently gather the dough together and lift out onto a lightly floured work surface. Press into a ball and flatten it slightly into a disc, wrap in plastic wrap and refrigerate for 30 minutes.

4 Preheat the oven to 200°C (400°F/Gas 6). Divide the pastry into six. Roll the dough out between two sheets of baking paper to fit six round 8 cm (3 in) fluted loose-bottomed tart tins, remove the top sheet of paper and invert the pastry into the tins. Use a small ball of pastry to help press the pastry into the tins, allowing any excess to hang over the sides. Roll the rolling pin over the tins to cut off any extra.

5 Line the pastry shells with a piece of crumpled baking paper large enough to cover the base and side of each tin and pour in some baking beads or (uncooked) rice. Bake for 10 minutes, then remove the paper and baking beads and return the pastry to the oven for 10 minutes, or until the base is dry and golden. Cool slightly. Reduce the oven to 180°C (350°F/Gas 4).

6 Heat the oil in a large frying pan, add the onion and cook over a medium heat for 20 minutes, or until the onion is caramelized. (Don't rush this step.)

7 Add the rocket and stir until wilted. Remove from the pan and cool.

8 Divide the onion mixture among the tart bases, then sprinkle with the blue cheese. Whisk together the eggs, cream, Parmesan cheese and nutmeg and pour evenly over each of the tarts. Place on a baking tray and bake for 20–30 minutes. Serve either hot or cold with a mixed green salad.

ASPARAGUS WITH POACHED QUAIL EGGS AND LIME HOLLANDAISE

SERVES 4 AS A STARTER

If you're serving brunch you could make this dish using chicken eggs, but for a special occasion, nothing beats the subtle delicacy of a quail egg.

Preparation time: 15 minutes
Total cooking time: 10 minutes

32 asparagus spears
2 tablespoons virgin olive oil
2 teaspoons cracked black pepper
2 teaspoons white vinegar
12 quail eggs
2 egg yolks
150 g (5½ oz) butter, melted
2 tablespoons lime juice
paprika, to serve
shavings of good-quality Parmesan
　　cheese, to serve

1　Trim the asparagus, brush with a little of the oil, then roll in the pepper, shaking off any excess.

2　Half-fill a deep frying pan with water and bring to a simmer, then add the vinegar—this will stop the egg white separating from the yolk as it cooks. Crack a quail egg into a small bowl before gently sliding it into the pan. Repeat with the other eggs. (You will probably need to cook them in two batches.) Cook for 1–2 minutes, or until the egg white turns opaque, then carefully remove from the pan with a spatula and keep warm.

3　Heat the remaining oil in a large frying pan and cook the asparagus over a high heat for 2–3 minutes, or until tender and bright green.

4　To make the hollandaise, place the egg yolks in a blender or whisk by hand and slowly add the melted butter in a thin, steady stream. Mix until all the butter has been added and the mixture has thickened slightly. Add the lime juice, season to taste with salt and cracked black pepper, then mix well.

5　Divide the asparagus among four warmed serving plates, top with three quail eggs per person, drizzle with some of the hollandaise and sprinkle with paprika and Parmesan cheese shavings. Best served immediately.

OYSTERS WITH FOUR TOPPINGS

Look for plump moist oysters with creamy flesh that smells of the sea.

Preparation time: 25 minutes
Total cooking time: 10 minutes

48 freshly shucked oysters
rock salt, to serve

TOMATO AND CORIANDER SALSA
2 small vine-ripened tomatoes
40 g (1½ oz) finely chopped red onion
1 tablespoon finely chopped
    coriander (cilantro) leaves
1 tablespoon rice vinegar
½ teaspoon caster (superfine) sugar

BLACK BEAN TOPPING
1½ tablespoons tinned salted
    black beans
2 teaspoons oil
1 garlic clove, crushed
1 spring onion (scallion), finely sliced
3 teaspoons soy sauce
3 teaspoons sherry
finely chopped red capsicum (pepper),
    to serve

CHILLI AND LIME SAUCE
1 teaspoon oil
1 garlic clove, crushed
2 teaspoons lime juice
1 tablespoon sweet chilli sauce
½ teaspoon sesame oil
1 teaspoon fish sauce
finely chopped Lebanese cucumber,
    to serve

GINGER AND SPRING ONION
    TOPPING
1 tablespoon Japanese soy sauce
2 teaspoons rice vinegar
3 teaspoons mirin
2 teaspoons thin strips fresh ginger
2 spring onions (scallions), thinly
    sliced on the diagonal

1 To make the tomato and coriander salsa, cut the tomatoes in half and remove the seeds with a teaspoon. Finely dice the tomato flesh and place in a small bowl with the red onion and chopped coriander leaves. Mix together well. Combine the rice vinegar and caster sugar in a jug, then stir into the tomato salsa. Season to taste with salt and cracked black pepper and refrigerate until ready to serve on the oysters.

2 To make the black bean topping, thoroughly wash the black beans under running water to remove any excess salt, then drain them. Roughly chop the beans and set aside. Heat the oil in a small saucepan over a medium heat, add the garlic and spring onion and cook for 30 seconds before adding the soy sauce, sherry and black beans. Simmer, stirring, for 2 minutes, or until the sauce has slightly thickened, then season to taste with salt and cracked black pepper. This topping is best served while warm.

3 To make the chilli and lime sauce, heat the oil in a small saucepan, add the garlic and cook for 1 minute, or until softened. Stir in the lime juice, sweet chilli sauce, sesame oil and fish sauce and simmer for a minute, or until just thickened. Allow to cool completely before serving.

4 To make the ginger and spring onion topping, combine the soy sauce, rice vinegar and mirin in a small saucepan and simmer over a low heat for 1 minute. Add the ginger and spring onion and simmer for a further 2 minutes. Serve warm.

To serve, sprinkle rock salt liberally on four plates. Place 12 oysters on each plate. Top three of the oysters on each plate with the tomato and coriander salsa. Spoon the black bean topping over another three, then sprinkle them with finely chopped red capsicum. Spoon chilli and lime sauce over three more oysters and top with some finely chopped cucumber. Drizzle the ginger and spring onion topping over the remaining three oysters. Serve immediately.

CHARGRILLED OCTOPUS SALAD

Baby octopus don't need tenderizing, but a good marinade will give the flesh extra flavour. Buy the octopus clean if you don't fancy cleaning them yourself.

Preparation time: 30 minutes + 2 hours refrigeration
Total cooking time: 15 minutes

1 kg (2 lb 4 oz) baby octopus
1 teaspoon sesame oil
2 tablespoons lime juice
2 tablespoons fish sauce
60 ml (¼ cup) sweet chilli sauce
200 g (4 handfuls) mixed salad
    leaves
1 red capsicum (pepper), very
    thinly sliced
2 small Lebanese cucumbers,
    seeded and cut into ribbons
4 red Asian shallots, chopped
100 g (3½ oz) toasted unsalted
    peanuts, chopped

1 To clean the octopus, remove the head from the tentacles by cutting just underneath the eyes. Carefully slit the head open and remove the gut. Cut it in half. Push out the beak from the centre of the tentacles, then cut the tentacles into sets of four or two, depending on their size. Pull the skin away from the head and tentacles if it comes away easily. The eyes will come off as you pull off the skin.

2 To make the marinade, combine the sesame oil, lime juice, fish sauce and sweet chilli sauce in a shallow non-metallic bowl. Add the octopus, and stir to coat. Cover and refrigerate for 2 hours.

3 Heat a chargrill pan (griddle) or barbecue to very hot. Drain the octopus, reserving the marinade, then cook in batches for 3–5 minutes, turning occasionally to ensure the octopus is evenly cooked.

4 Pour the marinade into a small saucepan, bring to the boil and cook for 2 minutes, or until it has slightly thickened.

5 Divide the salad leaves among four plates, scatter with capsicum and cucumber, then top with the octopus. Drizzle with the marinade and sprinkle with the red Asian shallots and peanuts.

TWICE-BAKED CHEESE SOUFFLES

SERVES 4 AS A STARTER

A high-riser that always impresses, soufflé literally means 'puffed up' in French. It's unlikely that these classics will ever let you down.

Preparation time: 30 minutes + 10 minutes standing + refrigeration
Total cooking time: 45 minutes

250 ml (1 cup) milk
2 cloves
1 onion, halved
3 black peppercorns
1 bay leaf
60 g (3 tablespoons) butter
30 g (1/4 cup) self-raising flour
2 eggs, at room temperature,
    separated
125 g (4 1/2 oz) Gruyère cheese, grated
250 ml (1 cup) cream
50 g (1/2 cup) grated Parmesan cheese

1 Preheat the oven to 180°C (350°F/Gas 4). Grease four 125 ml (1/2 cup) ramekins. Put the milk, clove-studded onion, peppercorns and bay leaf in a saucepan and heat until just about to boil, then remove from the heat and leave to cool for 10 minutes. Strain.

2 Melt the butter in a saucepan, add the flour and cook over a medium heat for 1 minute, or until golden. Remove from the heat and gradually stir in the milk, then return to the heat and stir constantly until the mixture boils and thickens. Simmer for 1 minute.

3 Transfer to a bowl, add the egg yolks and Gruyère cheese and mix.

4 Beat the egg whites in a clean dry bowl with a balloon whisk until soft peaks form, then gently fold into the milk mixture. Divide among the ramekins and run your finger around the rim to help the soufflés rise. Put the ramekins in a roasting tin with enough boiling water to come halfway up the sides of the dishes. Bake for 15–20 minutes, or until puffed. Remove, cool, then refrigerate for up to 2 days.

5 To serve, preheat the oven to 200°C (400°F/Gas 6), remove the soufflés from the ramekins and place each in a shallow ovenproof dish. Pour the cream over the top, sprinkle with Parmesan cheese and bake for 20 minutes, or until golden.

EGGPLANT STACKS WITH CAPSICUM, PESTO AND GOAT'S CHEESE

SERVES 4 AS A STARTER

Originally from India, eggplants or aubergines are now a popular vegetable around the world. Here, they've been given a Mediterranean makeover.

Preparation time: 20 minutes + 30 minutes standing
Total cooking time: 15 minutes

1 kg (2 lb 4 oz) eggplant (aubergine),
    cut into 12 slices (ends discarded)
1 large red capsicum (pepper)
olive oil, for pan-frying
45 g (1 handful) rocket leaves
100 g (3½ oz) goat's cheese
shredded rocket or basil, to garnish
balsamic vinegar, to serve (optional)
olive oil, to serve (optional)

PESTO
75 g (2 small handfuls) fresh basil
2 garlic cloves
2 tablespoons pine nuts, toasted
1 tablespoon lemon juice
1½ tablespoons grated Parmesan
    cheese
125 ml (½ cup) olive oil

1 Rub salt generously into the eggplant slices, then sit them in a colander for 30 minutes. Rinse under cold water and pat the eggplant dry.

2 Cut the capsicum into large pieces, removing the seeds and membrane. Put, skin-side-up, under a hot grill until the skin blackens and blisters. Cool in a plastic bag, then peel away the skin. Slice thinly.

3 To make the pesto, combine the basil, garlic, pine nuts, lemon juice and Parmesan cheese in a food processor or blender and process until minced. With the motor running, slowly pour in the oil and blend until smooth.

4 Lightly cover the base of a frying pan with oil and heat over a medium heat. Add the eggplant in batches and cook both sides until golden, adding more oil as needed. Drain on crumpled paper towels and keep warm.

5 To assemble, lay a few rocket leaves on a plate. Put one slice of eggplant on the rocket, then top with some more rocket leaves, a heaped teaspoon of pesto, one-eighth of the capsicum and one-eighth of the goat's cheese. Repeat, making two layers, and finish with a final slice of eggplant. Dollop some pesto on the top of the stack, sprinkle with shredded rocket or basil and season with pepper. Repeat, making three more stacks. Drizzle balsamic vinegar and olive oil around the plate, if desired. Serve immediately.

SCALLOPS ON ASIAN RISOTTO CAKES

SERVES 4 AS A STARTER

You don't have to serve these risotto cakes with scallops—they make an equally delicious vegetarian starter on their own with a dollop of pesto.

Preparation time: 35 minutes + 3 hours 10 minutes refrigeration
Total cooking time: 40 minutes

500 ml (2 cups) vegetable stock
2 tablespoons mirin
1 stalk lemon grass (white part only),
    bruised
2 kaffir lime leaves
3 coriander (cilantro) roots
2 tablespoons fish sauce
1 tablespoon butter
2–3 tablespoons oil
3 red Asian shallots, thinly sliced
4 spring onions (scallions), chopped
5 garlic cloves, chopped
2 1/4 tablespoons finely chopped
    fresh ginger
1 1/4 teaspoons white pepper
140 g (2/3 cup) risotto rice
2 tablespoons toasted unsalted
    chopped peanuts
50 g (1 handful) chopped coriander
    (cilantro) leaves
60 ml (1/4 cup) lime juice
1–2 teaspoons grated palm sugar
vegetable oil, for pan-frying
plain (all-purpose) flour, to dust
1 tablespoon oil, extra
16 large white scallops, cleaned and
    roes removed

1 Heat the stock, mirin, lemon grass, lime leaves, coriander roots, half the fish sauce and 250 ml (1 cup) of water in a saucepan, bring to the boil, then reduce the heat and keep at a low simmer.

2 Heat the butter and 1 tablespoon of the oil in a large saucepan over a medium heat until bubbling. Add the shallots, spring onions, 3 garlic cloves, 2 tablespoons of the ginger and 1 teaspoon of the pepper and cook for 2–3 minutes, or until fragrant and the onion is soft. Stir in the rice and toss until well coated.

3 Add 125 ml (1/2 cup) of the stock (avoid the lemon grass and coriander roots). Stir constantly over a medium heat until nearly all the liquid is absorbed. Continue adding the stock 125 ml (1/2 cup) at a time, stirring constantly, for 20–25 minutes, or until all the stock is absorbed and the rice is tender and creamy. Remove from the heat, cool, then cover and refrigerate for 3 hours, or until cold.

4 To make the pesto, combine the peanuts, coriander, remaining garlic, ginger and pepper in a blender or food processor and process until finely chopped. With the motor running, slowly add the lime juice, sugar and remaining fish sauce and oil and process until smooth—you might not need to use all the oil.

5 Divide the risotto into four balls, then mould into patties. Cover and refrigerate for 10 minutes. Heat the oil in a large frying pan over a medium heat. Dust the patties with flour and cook in batches for 2 minutes each side, or until crisp. Drain on paper towels. Cover and keep warm.

6 Heat the extra oil in a clean frying pan over a high heat. Cook the scallops in batches for 1 minute each side.

7 Serve each cake with four scallops, some pesto and lime wedges, if desired.

RICOTTA TARTS

SERVES 4 AS A STARTER

If you fancy a cheesy little Italian number, then this Mediterranean tart is hard to beat, with a flavour and texture that make it bellissimo in any language.

Preparation time: 20 minutes + 20 minutes cooling
Total cooking time: 30 minutes

35 g (1/3 cup) dry breadcrumbs
2 tablespoons virgin olive oil
1 garlic clove, crushed
1/2 red capsicum (pepper), quartered
    and cut into thin strips
1 zucchini (courgette), cut into
    thin strips
2 slices prosciutto, chopped
375 g (13 oz) firm ricotta cheese
40 g (1/3 cup) grated Cheddar
    cheese
40 g (1/3 cup) grated Parmesan
    cheese
2 tablespoons shredded basil
4 black olives, pitted and sliced

1 Preheat the oven to 180°C (350°F/Gas 4). Lightly grease four 8 cm (3 in) fluted tart tins. Lightly sprinkle 1 teaspoon of the breadcrumbs on the base and side of each tin.

2 To make the topping, heat half the oil in a frying pan, add the garlic, capsicum and zucchini and cook, stirring, over a medium heat for 5 minutes, or until the vegetables are soft. Remove from the heat and add the prosciutto. Season to taste with salt and cracked black pepper.

3 Take the ricotta (it must be firm or very well-drained or the tarts will be difficult to remove from their tins), and place it in a large bowl. Add the cheeses and remaining breadcrumbs. Season. Press the mixture into the tins and smooth the surface. Sprinkle with basil.

4 Scatter the topping over the ricotta mixture, top with the olives, then drizzle with the remaining oil.

5 Bake for 20 minutes, or until the tarts are slightly puffed and golden around the edges. Cool completely (the tarts will deflate on cooling) and carefully remove from the tins. Do not refrigerate.

DEEP-FRIED SQUID IN BESAN FLOUR BATTER WITH PARSLEY SALAD

SERVES 4 AS A STARTER

You can add bite to this seafood favourite by serving it with harissa—a hot chilli sauce made from a variety of spices and blended to a paste with red chillies and olive oil. Look for it in gourmet food shops.

Preparation time: 15 minutes + 30 minutes standing
Total cooking time: 10 minutes

DEEP-FRIED SQUID
150 g (5½ oz) besan (chickpea) flour
½ teaspoons paprika
1½ teaspoons ground cumin
½ teaspoon baking powder
250 ml (1 cup) soda water
oil, for deep-frying
6 squid, cleaned and sliced thinly
    into rings

PARSLEY SALAD
¼ preserved lemon, rinsed, pith
    and flesh removed
60 ml (¼ cup) lemon juice
60 ml (¼ cup) extra virgin olive oil
1 garlic clove, finely chopped
20 g (1 small handful) flat-leaf
    (Italian) parsley
harissa, to serve (optional)

1 To make the batter, sift the flour, paprika, cumin and baking powder into a bowl, add ¼ teaspoon pepper, mix together and make a well in the centre. Gradually add the soda water, whisking until smooth. Season with salt. Cover, then leave for 30 minutes.

2 Cut the lemon zest into very thin slivers. To make the dressing, whisk the lemon juice, extra virgin olive oil and garlic together in a bowl.

3 Fill a large heavy-based saucepan or wok one-third full of oil and heat until a cube of bread dropped into the oil browns in 15 seconds.

4 Dip the squid into the batter, allowing any excess to drip away. Cook in batches for 30–60 seconds, or until pale gold and crisp all over. Drain well on crumpled paper towels and keep warm.

5 Add the parsley and lemon slivers to the dressing, tossing to coat the leaves. Divide the leaves among four bowls or plates. Top with the squid rings and serve with harissa.

TEMPURA PRAWNS WITH SOBA NOODLES AND DASHI BROTH

SERVES 4 AS A STARTER

Made from dried bonito flakes and dried kelp, dashi is a soup stock commonly used in Japanese cooking. It's available in liquid, granulated or powdered form.

Preparation time: 20 minutes
Total cooking time: 15 minutes

200 g (7 oz) dried soba noodles
3 spring onions (scallions), sliced on
    the diagonal
60 g (⅓ cup) daikon, cut into
    thin strips
1 teaspoon dashi granules
60 ml (¼ cup) Japanese soy sauce
2 tablespoons mirin
½ teaspoon caster (superfine) sugar
2 teaspoons black sesame seeds
pickled ginger, to garnish

TEMPURA PRAWNS
12 raw king prawns (shrimps)
oil, for deep-frying
125 g (1 cup) tempura flour
250 ml (1 cup) iced water

1 Bring a large saucepan of water to the boil and cook the noodles for 5 minutes, or until al dente. Drain, then add the spring onions and daikon, toss well and keep warm.

2 To make the broth, put the dashi granules, soy sauce, mirin, sugar and 500 ml (2 cups) water in a saucepan and bring to the boil. Reduce the heat and simmer for 2–3 minutes. Remove from the heat, cover and keep warm.

3 To make the tempura prawns, peel and devein the prawns, keeping the tails intact. Make four incisions in the underside of each prawn.

4 Fill a wok or deep heavy-based saucepan one-third full of oil and heat until a cube of bread dropped into the oil browns in 15 seconds. Combine the tempura flour with the iced water and mix briefly with chopsticks or a fork—the batter should still be lumpy. Dip each prawn into the batter, leaving the tail uncoated. Deep-fry in batches for about 30 seconds, or until the prawns are light gold, crispy and cooked through. Drain well on crumpled paper towels.

5 Divide the noodles among four bowls and cover with broth, then top with the extra spring onion. Stand three prawns on top and sprinkle with sesame seeds. Garnish with pickled ginger and serve immediately.

WON TON CHICKEN RAVIOLI
WITH THAI DRESSING

SERVES 4 AS A STARTER

Won ton wrappers make an easy alternative to traditional pasta dough and can be used with any variety of fillings, whether Asian or Italian.

Preparation time: 35 minutes
Total cooking time: 15 minutes

400 g (14 oz) minced chicken
2 spring onions (scallions), finely
    chopped
3 kaffir lime leaves, very finely
    shredded
2 tablespoons sweet chilli sauce
4 tablespoons chopped coriander
    (cilantro) leaves
1½ teaspoons sesame oil
2 teaspoons grated lime zest
270 g (10 oz) packet won ton
    wrappers
125 ml (½ cup) fish sauce
2 tablespoons grated palm sugar
1 tablespoon oil
1 tablespoon lime juice
finely chopped red chilli, to garnish

1   Combine the chicken, spring onions, lime leaves, chilli sauce,
    3 tablespoons of the coriander, sesame oil and lime zest in a bowl.
2   Put a tablespoon of the mixture in the centre of a won ton wrapper, brush
    the edges lightly with water and top with another wrapper, pressing down
    around the edges to stop the ravioli from opening during cooking. Repeat
    with the remaining filling and wrappers.
3   Cook the ravioli in batches in a large saucepan of boiling water for
    5 minutes, or until al dente and the chicken is cooked, then drain well and
    put on serving plates.
4   Combine the fish sauce, palm sugar, oil and lime juice in a bowl. Pour over
    the ravioli and garnish with the chilli and remaining coriander.

MAIN COURSES

Cooking a special meal doesn't have to be stressful. It's fine to take short cuts if you need to—you can always buy good-quality ready-made tapenades and sauces if you simply don't have the time to make them fresh. Always read through the recipe to see if there's anything you can prepare beforehand, and that will leave you with more time to sit down and enjoy your guests as well as your food.

LEMON AND HERB RISOTTO
WITH FRIED MUSHROOMS

SERVES 4

You'll need to use a risotto rice such as arborio for this recipe as it releases starch during cooking that gives the dish the rich creaminess that it's renowned for.

Preparation time: 30 minutes
Total cooking time: 45 minutes

RISOTTO
1 litre (4 cups) chicken or vegetable
    stock
pinch saffron threads
2 tablespoons olive oil
2 leeks, thinly sliced
2 garlic cloves, crushed
440 g (2 cups) risotto rice
2–3 teaspoons finely grated
    lemon zest
2–3 tablespoons lemon juice
2 tablespoons chopped
    flat-leaf (Italian) parsley
2 tablespoons snipped chives
2 tablespoons chopped oregano
70 g (2½ oz) grated Parmesan
    cheese
100 g (3½ oz) mascarpone cheese

FRIED MUSHROOMS
30 g (1 oz) butter
1 tablespoon virgin olive oil
200 g (7 oz) small flat mushrooms,
    cut into thick slices
1 tablespoon balsamic vinegar

1 Bring the stock and saffron threads to the boil in a saucepan. Reduce the heat, cover and keep at a low simmer.

2 Heat the olive oil in a large saucepan over a medium heat. Add the leek, cook for 5 minutes, then add the garlic and cook for a further 5 minutes, or until golden. Add the rice and stir for 1 minute, or until the grains are well coated with the oil.

3 Add half the lemon zest and juice, then add 125 ml (½ cup) of the hot stock. Stir constantly over a medium heat until all the liquid has been absorbed. Continue adding more stock, 125 ml (½ cup) at a time, stirring constantly, for 25 minutes, or until the stock is absorbed and the rice is tender and creamy.

4 Stir in the parsley, chives, oregano, both cheeses and the remaining lemon zest and lemon juice, then remove from the heat, cover and keep warm.

5 To cook the mushrooms, melt the butter and virgin olive oil in a large frying pan, add the mushroom slices and vinegar and cook, stirring, over a high heat for 5–7 minutes, or until the mushrooms are tender and all the liquid has been absorbed.

6 Serve the risotto in large bowls topped with the mushrooms. Garnish with sprigs of fresh herbs, if desired.

SUMAC-CRUSTED LAMB FILLETS
WITH BABA GANOUJ

SERVES 4

Sumac is a ground-up berry that is used to infuse food with a lemon flavour without using any liquid. It's available from Middle Eastern grocery stores.

Preparation time: 15 minutes
Total cooking time: 25 minutes

2 tablespoons olive oil
750 g (1 lb 10 oz) small new
    potatoes
2–3 garlic cloves, crushed
60 ml (1/4 cup) lemon juice
1 red capsicum (pepper), seeded
    and quartered lengthways
4 x 200 g (7 oz) lamb backstraps
    or fillets
1 tablespoon sumac
3 tablespoons finely chopped
    flat-leaf (Italian) parsley
250 g (9 oz) good-quality
    baba ganouj

1 Heat the oil in a saucepan big enough to hold the potatoes in one layer. Add the potatoes and garlic, and cook, turning frequently, for 3–5 minutes, or until brown all over. When golden, add the lemon juice and reduce the heat. Gently simmer, covered, for 15–20 minutes, or until tender; stir occasionally to prevent sticking. Remove from the heat. Season well.

2 Meanwhile, lightly oil a chargrill pan (griddle) or barbecue plate and heat to very hot. Cook the capsicum pieces skin-side-down for 1–2 minutes, or until the skin starts to blister and turn black. Cook the other side for 1–2 minutes. Remove from the heat, then place in a plastic bag or bowl covered with plastic wrap. Set aside.

3 Coat the lamb with sumac (if sumac is unavailable, use cumin instead). Cook on the chargrill pan for 4–5 minutes on each side, or until cooked to your liking. Remove from the heat, cover with foil and leave to rest for a few minutes. Remove the skin from the capsicum and slice the quarters into thin strips.

4 Stir the parsley through the potatoes. Divide the baba ganouj among four plates. Cut the lamb into 1 cm (1/2 in) slices on the diagonal and arrange on top of the baba ganouj with the capsicum strips. Serve with the potatoes and a green salad.

PASTA WITH BABY SPINACH, ROASTED PUMPKIN AND TOMATO

SERVES 4

Marinated in oil, herbs and garlic, Persian feta is softer and creamier than other feta cheeses and adds a delicious saltiness to the pasta.

Preparation time: 15 minutes
Total cooking time: 1 hour

750 g (1 lb 10 oz) butternut or jap
   pumpkin (squash)
2 tablespoons Parmesan-cheese-
   infused olive oil
16 unpeeled garlic cloves
250 g (9 oz) cherry tomatoes, halved
500 g (1 lb 2 oz) orecchiette
   or penne
200 g (7 oz) baby English spinach
   leaves
200 g (7 oz) marinated Persian feta
   cheese
60 ml (1/4 cup) sherry vinegar
2 tablespoons walnut oil

1 Preheat the oven to 200°C (400°F/Gas 6). Cut the pumpkin into large cubes, put in a roasting tin and drizzle with Parmesan oil (available from gourmet food shops). Roast for 30 minutes, then add the garlic. Arrange the tomatoes on a baking tray. Put all the vegetables in the oven and roast for 10–15 minutes, or until cooked. Don't overcook the tomatoes or they will turn to mush.

2 Cook the pasta according to the packet instructions until al dente. Drain.

3 Toss together the pasta, tomatoes, pumpkin, garlic and spinach in a bowl.

4 Drain the feta and reserve 60 ml (1/4 cup) marinade. Whisk together the reserved marinade, vinegar and walnut oil. Pour over the pasta and sprinkle with pieces of the cheese.

DUCK BREAST ON SPICED COUSCOUS WITH RHUBARB RELISH

One of the most popular kinds of meat in China, duck can also be used in stir-fries, roasts and braised dishes. It's usually served with a tart fruit to cut through its rich flavour.

Preparation time: 20 minutes + 15 minutes standing
Total cooking time: 30 minutes

2½ tablespoons butter
1 tablespoon finely chopped
    French shallots
¼ teaspoon ground ginger
small pinch ground cloves
80 ml (⅓ cup) port
1 teaspoon red wine vinegar
1 tablespoon soft brown sugar
200 g (7 oz) rhubarb, thinly sliced
4 x 180 g (6 oz) duck breasts
1 teaspoon olive oil
375 ml (1½ cups) chicken stock
280 g (1½ cups) couscous
2 garlic cloves, crushed
1 teaspoon ground cumin
1 teaspoon ground cinnamon
20 g pistachio nuts, chopped
2 tablespoons finely chopped
    coriander (cilantro) leaves

1 To make the rhubarb relish, melt ½ tablespoon of the butter in a saucepan over a medium heat and cook the shallots for 4 minutes, or until softened. Add the ginger and cloves and stir for a further minute, or until fragrant. Stir in the port, vinegar and sugar and cook for 4 minutes, or until just syrupy, then add the rhubarb and cook for 4–5 minutes, or until just cooked through. Remove from the heat, cover and keep warm.

2 Season the duck breasts. Heat the oil in a large frying pan over a medium heat and cook the duck breasts, skin-side-down, for 7 minutes, or until the skin is golden, then turn and cook for a further 2 minutes, or until tender. Flip the breasts over again, increase the heat to high and cook for 1 minute longer to make the skin crispy. Remove from the heat, cover loosely with foil and rest for 10 minutes.

3 Boil the stock in a saucepan over a high heat. Remove from the heat and stir in the couscous. Put the lid on the pan and leave for 5 minutes.

4 Melt the remaining butter in a small saucepan, add the garlic and spices and stir over a medium heat for 1 minute. Remove the lid from the couscous, add the butter and spice mix and mix in with a fork. Stir in the pistachios and coriander. Gently reheat the rhubarb if necessary.

5 Spoon a mound of couscous onto four serving plates, top with the duck breasts and some rhubarb relish.

TUNA STEAKS ON CORIANDER NOODLES

SERVES 4

If you prefer, you can serve the tuna steaks whole rather than cutting them into cubes. If you do serve them whole, the dish would look better with the noodles placed on the side.

Preparation time: 15 minutes
Total cooking time: 10 minutes

60 ml (1/4 cup) lime juice
2 tablespoons fish sauce
2 tablespoons sweet chilli sauce
2 teaspoons grated palm sugar
1 teaspoon sesame oil
1 garlic clove, finely chopped
1 tablespoon virgin olive oil
4 x 150 g (51/2 oz) tuna steaks, at
    room temperature
200 g (7 oz) dried thin wheat
    noodles
6 spring onions (scallions),
    thinly sliced
25 g (3/4 cup) chopped coriander
    (cilantro) leaves
lime wedges, to garnish

1 To make the dressing, place the lime juice, fish sauce, chilli sauce, sugar, sesame oil and garlic in a small bowl and mix together.

2 Heat the olive oil in a chargrill pan (griddle) or barbecue. Add the tuna steaks and cook over a high heat for 2 minutes each side, or until cooked to your liking. Transfer the steaks to a warm plate, cover and keep warm.

3 Put the noodles in a large saucepan of lightly salted, rapidly boiling water and return to the boil. Cook for 4 minutes, or until the noodles are tender. Drain well. Add half the dressing and half the spring onion and coriander to the noodles and gently toss together.

4 Either cut the tuna into even cubes or slice it.

5 Put the noodles on serving plates and top with the tuna. Mix the remaining dressing with the spring onion and coriander and drizzle over the tuna. Garnish with lime wedges.

SIDE SALADS

Whatever main course you serve, you'll need a salad on the side to complement it. Try one—or several—of these fresh ideas.

COUSCOUS SALAD

Prepare 500 g (1 lb 2 oz) couscous according to the packet instructions. Put in a large bowl and add 1 chopped red onion, 200 g (7 oz) cubed feta cheese, 60 g (1/2 cup) sliced black olives, 2 peeled, seeded and chopped small cucumbers and 50 g (1 handful) chopped mint. Whisk together 125 ml (1/2 cup) olive oil and 125 ml (1/2 cup) lemon juice and toss through. Serves 6.

FETA, BEETROOT AND ROCKET SALAD

Drain two 340 g (12 oz) jars baby beetroots and cut into quarters. Put in a large serving bowl with 200 g (7 oz) rocket (arugula) leaves and 300 g (10 1/2 oz) drained and cubed marinated feta cheese. Put 60 ml (1/4 cup) olive oil and 1 tablespoon balsamic vinegar in a small bowl and mix together well, then pour over the salad and toss well. Season with black pepper. Serves 6.

SEMI-DRIED TOMATO AND ENGLISH SPINACH SALAD

Remove and discard the pith and flesh from 2 quarters of preserved lemon. Wash the zest and thinly slice. Put 150 g (3 handfuls) English spinach leaves in a bowl with 200 g (7 oz) sliced semi-dried (sun-blushed) tomatoes, a 225 g (8 oz) jar drained and sliced marinated artichoke hearts, 85 g (1/2 cup) small black olives and the preserved lemon slices. Put 2 tablespoons lemon juice, 3 tablespoons olive oil and 1 large crushed garlic clove in a bowl, season and mix well. Pour over the spinach mixture and toss to coat. Serve immediately. Serves 6.

BEAN SALAD WITH GARLIC DRESSING

Bring a saucepan of lightly salted water to the boil. Add 250 g (9 oz) green beans and 250 g (9 oz) yellow beans and cook for 2 minutes, or until just tender. Plunge into cold water and drain. Put 60 ml (1/4 cup) olive oil, 1 tablespoon lemon juice and 1 crushed garlic clove in a bowl, season with salt and freshly ground black pepper, and mix together well. Put the beans in a serving bowl, pour on the dressing and toss to coat. Top with shaved Parmesan cheese and serve. Serves 6.

ROAST TOMATO AND BASIL SALAD

Cut 6 Roma (plum) tomatoes in quarters lengthways. Put on a grill tray, skin-side-down, and cook under a hot grill for 4–5 minutes, or until golden. Cool to room temperature. Put in a bowl. Combine 2 teaspoons capers, 6 torn basil leaves, 1 tablespoon olive oil, 1 tablespoon balsamic vinegar, 2 crushed garlic cloves and 1/2 teaspoon honey in a bowl, season with salt and freshly ground black pepper, and pour over the tomatoes. Toss gently. Serves 6.

CREAMY POTATO SALAD

Boil 1 kg (2 lb 4 oz) washed kipfler potatoes, or other waxy potatoes, for 20 minutes, or until tender. Cut into 3 cm (1 in) slices on the diagonal. Cook 125 g (4 1/2 oz) chopped bacon in a little oil until crispy and golden. Add to the potatoes with 2 chopped spring onions (scallions). Whisk together 125 g (1/2 cup) sour cream, 2 tablespoons each olive oil and red wine vinegar and 2 teaspoons each Dijon and wholegrain mustard. Pour the dressing over the potatoes and gently toss to combine. Season with freshly ground black pepper. Serves 6.

Opposite page top to bottom:
Couscous salad, Feta, beetroot and rocket salad, Semi-dried tomato and English spinach salad.
This page top to bottom:
Bean salad with garlic dressing, Roast tomato and basil salad, Creamy potato salad.

CORN-FED CHICKEN BREASTS
WITH LENTILS AND STAR ANISE JUS

SERVES 4

Most supermarkets today stock a variety of chickens from free-range to organic to corn-fed, but if the sort you're after isn't available, ask your butcher.

Preparation time: 20 minutes + 10 minutes standing
Total cooking time: 2 hour 40 minutes

600 g (1 lb 5 oz) raw chicken
    carcasses
2 onions
2 carrots
2 celery stalks
80 ml (1/3 cup) olive oil
2 star anise
3 garlic cloves
4 sprigs of thyme
170 g (3/4 cup) puy lentils
1 bay leaf
1 tablespoon chopped thyme
4 corn-fed chicken breast fillets
    (with or without wing bone)

1 To make the jus, chop the carcasses into large pieces. Roughly chop one onion, carrot and celery stalk. Heat 1 tablespoon of the oil in a very large saucepan over a medium heat. Add the chopped vegetables and cook for about 4 minutes, or until they start to brown, then remove from the pan. Add another tablespoon of the oil and the chicken bones to the pan and cook, stirring, for about 5 minutes, or until well browned. Return the vegetables to the pan and add the star anise, 2 bruised garlic cloves, the thyme and 2.5 litres (10 cups) cold water. Bring to the boil, reduce the heat and simmer for 1 1/2 hours, removing any scum that forms on the top.

2 Strain into a clean saucepan and simmer over a medium heat for 1 hour, or until slightly thick—you should have 170 ml (2/3 cup) jus. Remove from the heat, cover and keep warm.

3 Meanwhile, prepare the rest of the meal. Rinse the lentils under running water, then put in a large saucepan and cover with cold water. Bring slowly to the boil, then simmer over a medium heat for 20–25 minutes, or until tender but not mushy. Drain. Finely chop the remaining onion and dice the carrot and celery stalk.

4 Heat another tablespoon of the oil in a large frying pan over a medium heat, add the bay leaf and onion and cook for 3 minutes, then add the carrot and celery and cook for 5 minutes, stirring, until softened and lightly browned. Stir in the remaining garlic clove, crushed, and the chopped thyme and cook for 1 minute. Gently fold in the lentils, stirring carefully for 2 minutes to heat through. Season, then remove from the heat and cover with foil to keep warm.

5 Heat the remaining oil in a large frying pan over a high heat. Season the chicken breasts with salt and black pepper, then cook, skin-side-down, for 5 minutes. Turn over, reduce the heat to medium and cook for a further 5 minutes, or until tender. Remove from the heat and rest for 10 minutes.

6 Put a mound of lentils on each plate, top with the chicken and spoon the jus around the plate.

SALMON WITH ASIAN GREENS AND CHILLI JAM

SERVES 4

Salmon cutlets are ideal to pan-fry, requiring just a couple of minutes on each side, which leaves you plenty of time to enjoy your own party.

Preparation time: 20 minutes
Total cooking time: 1 hour

1 tablespoon oil
1 red capsicum (pepper),
    thinly sliced
500 g (1 lb 2 oz) baby bok choy
    (pak choi), quartered
1 garlic clove, finely chopped
1 tablespoon soy sauce
1 teaspoon sugar
1 tablespoon oil, for
    pan-frying
4 x 150–200 g (5½–7 oz) salmon
    cutlets

CHILLI JAM
2½ tablespoons oil
1 large onion, thinly sliced
6 red bird's-eye chillies, seeded
    and thinly sliced
2 teaspoons grated fresh ginger
185 ml (¾ cup) white wine vinegar
140 g (¾ cup) soft brown sugar
2 teaspoons lime juice

1 To make the chilli jam, heat the oil in a saucepan and add the onion, chilli and ginger. Cook over a medium heat for 3–4 minutes, or until the onion is soft. Add the remaining ingredients and 60 ml (¼ cup) water and stir until the sugar dissolves. Bring to the boil, then reduce the heat and simmer for 35–40 minutes, or until thick and pulpy (it will thicken as it cools). Cool slightly, transfer to a food processor, then process until smooth. Cool.

2 Heat the oil in a frying pan, add the capsicum and cook over a medium heat for 2 minutes, or until softened slightly, then add the bok choy and cook for 1 minute, or until wilted. Add the garlic and cook until fragrant. Reduce the heat, add the soy sauce and sugar and warm gently. Remove from the heat and keep warm.

3 Heat the vegetable oil in a frying pan, season the salmon and cook over a medium heat for 2 minutes each side, or until cooked to your liking. It should be just rare in the centre—do not overcook or the flesh will dry out.

4 Divide the vegetables among four plates and top with a salmon cutlet. Dollop with chilli jam and serve.

SPATCHCOCK WITH ZUCCHINI PANCAKES AND RELISH

SERVES 4

A spatchcock, also known as a poussin, is a very young chicken. The term also refers to the method of splitting it down the back and flattening it ready for the grill.

Preparation time: 30 minutes + overnight refrigeration + 40 minutes standing
Total cooking time: 1 hour

60 g (1 large handful) finely
    chopped basil
2 garlic cloves, crushed
2 teaspoons grated lemon zest
60 ml (1/4 cup) olive oil
4 spatchcocks

ZUCCHINI PANCAKES
700 g (1 lb 9 oz) zucchini
    (courgettes)
4 eggs
40 g (1 1/2 oz) Parmesan cheese,
    grated
40 g (1/3 cup) plain (all-purpose)
    flour
1 garlic clove, crushed
A few sprigs chopped
    flat-leaf (Italian) parsley
2 tablespoons olive oil

TOMATO AND BLACK OLIVE
    RELISH
2 large ripe tomatoes, seeded and
    diced
60 g (1/2 cup) sliced black olives
1 1/2 tablespoons extra virgin olive oil
2 garlic cloves, crushed
2 tablespoons finely chopped
    flat-leaf (Italian) parsley

1 Put the basil, garlic, lemon zest, 1 teaspoon of salt and 1/2 teaspoon of cracked black pepper in a large non-metallic dish and mix. Whisk in the oil. Rub under and over the spatchcock skin. Cover and refrigerate overnight.

2 Slice both ends off the zucchini but don't peel. Grate on the coarse side of a grater. Toss with salt and sit in a colander for 30 minutes.

3 Preheat the oven to 190°C (375°F/Gas 5). Grease a large chargrill pan (griddle) or barbecue and cook the spatchcocks one or two at a time over a medium heat for 5 minutes each side, or until golden. Transfer to a large roasting tin and roast for 10–12 minutes, or until the juices run clear when the inside of a thigh is pierced. Remove from the oven, cover with foil and rest for 10 minutes.

4 Rinse the salt off the zucchini and squeeze to remove any excess liquid. Mix the zucchini with the eggs, Parmesan cheese, flour, garlic, parsley and 1 teaspoon of salt. Season to taste with pepper. Heat half the oil in a non-stick frying pan over a medium heat. Form two pancakes (each using about 3 tablespoons of batter) and cook for 2 1/2 minutes each side, or until golden. Drain on paper towels and repeat with the remaining oil and batter to make six more pancakes.

5 To make the relish, combine all the ingredients in a bowl. Season to taste.

6 Carve the spatchcock into four and serve with two zucchini cakes and a dollop of the relish.

CHICKEN WITH CORIANDER CHUTNEY AND SPICED EGGPLANT

SERVES 4

As it's served on naan, the best way to eat this is the Indian way—picked up in your fingers.

Preparation time: 1 hour 10 minutes + overnight refrigeration + 30 minutes soaking
Total cooking time: 1 hour 10 minutes

250 g (1 cup) plain yoghurt
1 tablespoon lemon juice
1/2 onion, coarsely chopped
2 garlic cloves, finely chopped
2 teaspoons chopped fresh ginger
1/2 teaspoon ground cumin
750 g (1 lb 10 oz) chicken thighs,
    trimmed and cut into
    4 cm (1 1/2 in) cubes
4 pieces ready-made naan
plain yoghurt, to serve

SPICED EGGPLANT
1 large eggplant (aubergine)
2 tablespoons oil
1 onion, finely chopped
3 teaspoons chopped fresh ginger
2 garlic cloves, crushed
1/2 teaspoon ground turmeric
1 teaspoon ground cumin
1 tomato, finely diced
2 teaspoons lemon juice

CORIANDER CHUTNEY
60 ml (1/4 cup) lemon juice
100 g (2 handfuls) coarsely chopped
    fresh coriander (cilantro) leaves
    and stems
35 g (1/4 cup) finely chopped onion
1 tablespoon chopped fresh ginger
1/2 jalapeño pepper, seeded and finely
    chopped
1 teaspoon sugar

1 Combine the yoghurt, lemon juice, onion, garlic, ginger and cumin in a large non-metallic bowl, add the chicken and toss. Cover and refrigerate overnight.

2 Preheat the oven to 240°C (475°F/Gas 9). Soak eight wooden skewers in water for 30 minutes. To make the purée, prick the eggplant in a few places, put on a baking tray and bake for 35–40 minutes, or until soft and wrinkled. Cool. Reduce the oven to 200°C (400°F/Gas 6).

3 Meanwhile, to make the chutney, put the lemon juice, coriander and 60 ml (1/4 cup) of water in a food processor and process until smooth. Add the remaining ingredients and season.

4 When the eggplant is cool enough to handle, cut in half, scoop out the flesh and coarsely chop. Heat the oil in a frying pan over a medium heat. Add the onion and cook for 5 minutes, or until soft. Add the ginger and garlic and cook for 2 minutes, or until fragrant. Add the spices and cook for 1 minute, then add the tomato and 60 ml (1/4 cup) of water and simmer for 5 minutes, or until the tomato is soft and the mixture is thick. Stir in the eggplant and lemon juice and season. Cook for 2 minutes, then remove from the heat and keep warm.

5 Thread the chicken onto skewers and chargrill over a medium heat for 4–6 minutes each side, or until tender.

6 Meanwhile, heat the naan in the oven for 5 minutes. Reheat the eggplant over a low heat if needed. Place the naan on a plate and spread a quarter of the eggplant in the centre, leaving a 4 cm (1 1/2 in) border. Lay two chicken skewers on top and drizzle with chutney and yoghurt.

SPAGHETTINI WITH ASPARAGUS AND ROCKET

SERVES 4

You can use whatever pasta you like in this dish—you'll find that the sauce goes equally well on tagliatelle, macaroni or spirals.

Preparation time: 15 minutes
Total cooking time: 15 minutes

100 ml (½ cup) extra virgin olive oil
16 thin asparagus spears, cut into
    5 cm (2½ in) lengths
375 g (13 oz) spaghettini
120 g (2 large handfuls) rocket
    (arugula), shredded
2 small red chillies, finely chopped
2 teaspoons finely grated lemon zest
1 garlic clove, finely chopped
100 g (1 cup) grated Parmesan
    cheese
2 tablespoons lemon juice

1 Bring a large saucepan of water to the boil over a medium heat. Add 1 tablespoon of the oil and a pinch of salt to the water and blanch the asparagus for 3–4 minutes. Remove the asparagus with a slotted spoon, refresh under cold water, drain and place in a bowl. Return the water to a rapid boil and add the spaghettini. Cook the pasta according to the packet instructions until al dente. Drain and return to the pan.

2 Meanwhile, add the rocket, chilli, lemon rind, garlic and 65 g (⅔ cup) of the Parmesan cheese to the asparagus and mix well. Add the mixture to the cooked pasta, pour on the lemon juice and the remaining olive oil and season with salt and freshly ground black pepper. Stir well to evenly coat the pasta with the mixture. Divide among four pasta bowls, top with the remaining cheese and serve.

TAPENADE LAMB RACKS WITH FETA AND COUSCOUS

SERVES 4

A couple of tips when you make this dish: Bulgarian feta cheese has a distinctive flavour, but you can use normal feta if you prefer. To save time, pick up a jar of good-quality ready-made olive tapenade.

Preparation time: 30 minutes + 15 minutes standing
Total cooking time: 1 hour 10 minutes

2 teaspoons capers
15 g (1/2 oz) drained anchovy fillets
1 garlic clove
90 g (3/4 cup) sliced pitted black
  olives
1 1/2 tablespoons lemon juice
1 1/2 tablespoons extra virgin olive oil
1 tablespoon Cognac
8 small ripe Roma (plum) tomatoes,
  halved
150 g (5 1/2 oz) Bulgarian feta cheese
4 lamb racks with 3 cutlets each
375 ml (1 1/2 cups) chicken stock
1 tablespoon olive oil
1 red onion, thinly sliced
1 tablespoon baby capers
185 g (1 cup) couscous
1 teaspoon orange zest
25 g (1 oz) butter
1 1/2 tablespoons chopped mint

1 Preheat the oven to 180°C (350°F/Gas 4). To make the tapenade, put the capers, anchovy fillets, garlic, olives and lemon juice in a food processor or blender and process until finely chopped. While the motor is running, slowly pour in the extra virgin olive oil and Cognac. Season with pepper. If you're using ready-made tapenade, you'll need 155 g (1/2 cup).

2 Put the tomatoes on a wire rack in a roasting tin, sprinkle with salt and pepper and roast for 40 minutes, or until slightly dried. Sprinkle with the crumbled feta cheese. Increase the oven to 220°C (425°F/Gas 7).

3 Trim and clean the lamb racks, then coat them in the tapenade and put in a roasting tin. Cook for 20–25 minutes, or until cooked to your liking. Rest for 10 minutes before carving into cutlets.

4 Bring the chicken stock to the boil in a saucepan. Meanwhile, heat the olive oil in a frying pan, add the onion and baby capers and cook over a medium heat for 5 minutes, or until the onion is tender. Transfer to a bowl, add the couscous, orange zest and butter and cover with the boiling stock. Leave for 5 minutes, or until all the liquid has been absorbed. Fluff with a fork to separate the grains, adding half the mint.

5 To serve, put a mound of couscous in the centre of four serving plates. Top with a cutlet, then a piece of tomato, another cutlet, another tomato half and finish with a cutlet. Lean two pieces of tomato up against the side of each stack, sprinkle with the remaining mint and serve.

STEAMED CHICKEN WITH
LEMON GRASS, GINGER AND ASIAN GREENS

For healthy food with plenty of taste, it's hard to go past an Asian-style meal that uses a low-fat method of cooking such as steaming, and a variety of fresh herbs for flavour.

Preparation time: 25 minutes
Total cooking time: 40 minutes

200 g (7 oz) fresh egg noodles
4 chicken breast fillets
2 stalks lemon grass
5 cm (2 in) piece fresh ginger, cut
    into julienne strips
1 lime, thinly sliced
500 ml (2 cups) chicken stock
350 g (1 bunch) choy sum, cut into
    10 cm (4 in) lengths
800 g (1 lb 12 oz) Chinese broccoli,
    cut into 10 cm (4 in) lengths
60 ml (¼ cup) kecap manis
60 ml (¼ cup) soy sauce
1 teaspoon oil
toasted sesame seeds, to garnish

1 Cook the egg noodles in a saucepan of boiling water for 5 minutes, then drain and keep warm.
2 Cut each chicken breast fillet horizontally through the middle so that you are left with eight thin flat fillets.
3 Cut the lemon grass into lengths that are about 5 cm (2 in) longer than the chicken fillets, then cut in half lengthways. Put one piece of lemon grass onto one half of each chicken breast fillet, top with some ginger and lime slices, then top with the other half of the fillet.
4 Pour the stock into a wok and bring to a simmer. Put two of the chicken fillets in a paper-lined bamboo steamer. Put the steamer over the wok and steam over the simmering stock for 12–15 minutes, or until the chicken is tender. Remove the chicken from the steamer, cover and keep warm. Repeat with the other fillets.
5 Steam the greens in the same way for 3 minutes, or until tender. Bring the stock in the wok to the boil.
6 Put the kecap manis, soy sauce and sesame oil in a bowl and whisk together well.
7 Divide the noodles among four serving plates and ladle the boiling stock over them. Top with a neat pile of Asian greens, then add the chicken and generously drizzle each serve with the sauce. Sprinkle with toasted sesame seeds and serve.

LEMON CHICKEN ON BASIL MASH
WITH GARLIC LEMON AIOLI

SERVES 4

It's easy to make a comfort food like mashed potato into something special by adding a scoop of sour cream and a handful of fresh basil or parsley.

Preparation time: 20 minutes + overnight refrigeration
Total cooking time: 25 minutes

60 ml (1/4 cup) lemon juice
4 garlic cloves, crushed
80 ml (1/3 cup) olive oil
4 x 150 g (5 1/2 oz) corn-fed chicken
   breast fillets, skin on
90 g (1/3 cup) whole-egg
   mayonnaise
1 tablespoon lemon juice, extra
800 g (1 lb 12 oz) desiree potatoes,
   cut into large chunks
1 1/2 tablespoons butter
90 g (1/3 cup) sour cream
1 teaspoon sea salt flakes
2 tablespoons finely shredded basil

1 Combine the lemon juice, 2 garlic cloves and half the olive oil in a non-metallic flat dish. Coat the chicken in the marinade, then cover with plastic wrap and refrigerate overnight.

2 To make the aïoli, combine the mayonnaise, extra lemon juice and 1 garlic clove in a small bowl, then season to taste. Cover.

3 Cook the potato in a saucepan of boiling water for 12 minutes, or until soft. Drain, then return to the heat until all the moisture has been absorbed. Add the butter, sour cream, sea salt and remaining garlic and mash with a potato masher until smooth and lump free. Remove from the heat and cover.

4 Meanwhile, drain the chicken. Heat the remaining oil in a large frying pan over a medium heat until sizzling. Add the chicken, skin-side-down, and cook for 4–5 minutes, or until the skin is golden and crispy, then turn and cook for 5 minutes, or until tender and cooked through. Leave chicken breasts to rest for 5 minutes.

5 Stir the shredded basil through the mash just before serving.

6 To serve, put a dollop of mash on the centre of each plate, top with a chicken breast, then some aïoli. Season and serve with a crisp green salad.

BEEF FILLET WITH ONION MARMALADE AND CREAMY POTATO GRATIN

SERVES 4

This is the sort of dinner that's perfect during the winter months—a grown-up version of steak and potatoes that never goes out of fashion.

Preparation time: 30 minutes + 2 hours refrigeration
Total cooking time: 1 hour 10 minutes

250 ml (1 cup) port
60 ml (1/4 cup) balsamic vinegar
2 garlic cloves, crushed
4 beef eye fillet steaks
1 tablespoon olive oil

ONION MARMALADE
60 ml (1/4 cup) olive oil
500 g (1 lb 2 oz) onions, thinly sliced
45 g (1/4 cup) soft brown sugar
75 ml (1/3 cup) red wine vinegar

POTATO GRATIN
4 large potatoes, thinly sliced
1 onion, thinly sliced
250 ml (1 cup) cream
50 g (1³/4 oz) Gruyère cheese,
    grated

1 Put the port, vinegar and garlic in a non-metallic dish and mix together well. Add the beef and stir to coat. Cover and refrigerate for 2 hours. Drain, reserving the marinade.

2 To make the onion marmalade, heat the olive oil in a large non-stick frying pan, add the onion and sugar and cook over a medium heat for 30–40 minutes, or until caramelized. Stir in the red wine vinegar, bring the mixture to the boil and cook for 10 minutes, or until thick and sticky. Remove from the heat and keep warm.

3 Meanwhile, preheat the oven to 180°C (350°F/Gas 4). Lightly grease four 125 ml (1/2 cup) soufflé dishes, then fill with alternating layers of potato and onion. Mix the cream and cheese together in a bowl and season, then pour into the dishes. Place on a baking tray and bake for 45 minutes, or until the potato is cooked. Turn the oven off. Keep warm.

4 Heat the oil in a large frying pan, add the steaks and cook over a high heat for 3–5 minutes each side, or until cooked to your liking. Remove from the pan and keep warm, then add the reserved marinade to the pan and boil for 5–6 minutes, or until reduced by half.

5 Spoon some of the sauce onto four serving plates, place a steak on the sauce, top with a generous mound of onion marmalade and a gratin. Serve with steamed greens.

PROSCIUTTO-WRAPPED PORK
WITH POLENTA

SERVES 4

Sage has a powerful flavour that goes particularly well with fatty meats such as pork, goose or duck. Tucking it in between the pork and prosciutto means it will flavour both.

Preparation time: 25 minutes + 10 minutes resting
Total cooking time: 40 minutes

8 slices prosciutto
4 x 200 g (7 oz) thin pork fillets
24 large sage leaves
2 tablespoons olive oil
250 ml (1 cup) verjuice or
    white wine
2 tablespoons balsamic vinegar
200 g (7 oz) cherry tomatoes
70 g (2½ oz) butter
1 litre (4 cups) chicken stock
170 g (1 cup) fine instant polenta
100 g (3½ oz) mascarpone cheese
45 g (½ cup) grated pecorino
    cheese

1 Preheat the oven to 200°C (400°F/Gas 6). Wrap two slices of prosciutto around each pork fillet, tucking in three sage leaves as you go. Secure the sage leaves in place with toothpicks.

2 Heat the oil in a frying pan over a high heat and cook the pork in batches for 3 minutes, or until golden, then transfer to a baking dish. Deglaze the pan by adding the verjuice and vinegar and scraping up any sediment. Pour the pan juices over the pork, bake for 10 minutes, then cover and rest for 10 minutes. (Leave the oven on.)

3 Lay out the tomatoes in a roasting tin and roast for 10 minutes, or until tender. Keep the tomatoes warm.

4 Meanwhile, brush both sides of the remaining sage leaves with 1 tablespoon of melted butter, lay on a baking tray and bake for 5 minutes, or until crisp.

5 Bring the stock to the boil in a large saucepan, then slowly add the polenta, stirring constantly. Cook, stirring, for 8–10 minutes, or until smooth and thick. Stir in the remaining butter, mascarpone and pecorino and season.

6 Lay slices of pork on a bed of polenta, drizzle with the cooking juices and top with the tomatoes. Scatter with the sage leaves and serve.

LAMB CUTLETS WITH BEETROOT, BEAN AND POTATO SALAD

SERVES 4

Although beetroot has long been popular in eastern Europe—it is the main ingredient in the Russian soup, borscht—its rise in popularity elsewhere is more recent, and very much overdue.

Preparation time: 15 minutes + overnight refrigeration
Total cooking time: 35 minutes

2 garlic cloves, crushed
2 tablespoons finely chopped thyme
1½ tablespoons lemon juice
1 tablespoon walnut oil
2 tablespoons extra virgin
   olive oil
12 lamb cutlets, trimmed
6 baby beetroot, trimmed
500 g (1 lb 2 oz) kipfler potatoes,
   unpeeled
250 g (9 oz) baby green beans
2 tablespoons olive oil

DRESSING
1 garlic clove, crushed
3½ tablespoons lemon juice
80 ml (⅓ cup) extra virgin
   olive oil
1 tablespoon walnut oil
30 g (¼ cup) chopped walnuts

1 Combine the garlic, thyme, lemon juice, walnut oil and extra virgin olive oil in a shallow, non-metallic dish, add the cutlets and toss well. Cover with plastic wrap and refrigerate overnight.

2 Cook the beetroot in boiling water for 20 minutes, or until tender. Drain. Meanwhile, cook the potatoes in lightly salted boiling water for 12 minutes, or until tender. Drain.

3 When cool enough to handle, peel the beetroot and potatoes. Cut each beetroot into six wedges and thickly slice the potatoes.

4 Cook the beans in lightly salted boiling water for 4 minutes. Drain, refresh under cold water, then drain again. Pat dry with paper towels.

5 Heat the olive oil in a large frying pan over a high heat and cook the cutlets in batches for 4–5 minutes, or until cooked to your liking, turning once.

6 Whisk the garlic, lemon juice, extra virgin olive oil and walnut oil in a large bowl. Add the potatoes, beans and walnuts and toss gently. Season and arrange over the beetroot. Top with the cutlets and serve.

VEGETABLES ON THE SIDE

It's easy to serve vegetables that are just as delicious as the main dish.

CITRUS-GLAZED CARROTS

Trim the tops from 1 kg (2 lb 4 oz) baby carrots. Place 20 g (1 tablespoon) butter in a small saucepan and melt, add 2 teaspoons honey, 1 tablespoon orange juice, 2 teaspoons grated orange zest and the carrots, and toss through. Cook, covered, over a medium heat for 4–5 minutes, or until tender. Sprinkle with chopped flat-leaf (Italian) parsley, season and serve immediately. Serves 4–6.

ROASTED TOMATOES WITH BALSAMIC AND BASIL

Preheat the oven to 170°C (325°F/Gas 3). Cut 6 Roma (plum) tomatoes in half lengthways and place on a lightly greased baking tray, skin-side-down. Mix 60 ml (1/4 cup) olive oil with 2 tablespoons balsamic vinegar and drizzle over the tomato halves. Bruise 5 unpeeled garlic cloves with the back of a knife and scatter over the baking tray between the tomatoes. Sprinkle 1 1/2 teaspoons sugar over the tomatoes, then cook in the oven for 35–40 minutes, or until quite soft. Arrange the tomatoes on a serving plate, scatter with the roasted garlic and top each tomato half with a small basil leaf. Drizzle with any remaining pan juices and season. Serves 4–6.

BAKED SWEET POTATO CHIPS

Preheat the oven to 190°C (375°F/Gas 5). Peel 700 g (1 lb 9 oz) orange sweet potato and slice very thinly. Place in a large bowl, add 60 ml (1/4 cup) extra virgin olive oil and 2 teaspoons cumin seeds, and toss well to coat evenly. Place on a baking-paper-lined baking tray in a single layer and bake for 45 minutes, or until crisp and golden. Season with salt and serve immediately. Serves 4.

MIXED STEAMED ASIAN GREENS

Place 750 ml (3 cups) water, 1 thinly sliced lime and 1 tablespoon chopped fresh ginger in a wok or large saucepan and bring to the boil. Place a bamboo steamer lined with baking paper over the wok and add 500 g (1 lb 2 oz) trimmed mixed Asian greens, such as bok choy (pak choi), choy sum, snake beans or Chinese broccoli. Steam for 2–3 minutes, or until tender. Toss through 1/2 teaspoon sesame oil and sprinkle with 2 teaspoons toasted sesame seeds. Serves 4–6.

SAFFRON MASHED POTATO

Chop 1 kg (2 lb 4 oz) peeled floury potatoes into cubes. Place in a large saucepan with 500 ml (2 cups) chicken stock and 500 ml (2 cups) water. Bring to the boil, then reduce the heat and simmer for 15 minutes, or until soft. Drain, reserving 60 ml (1/4 cup) cooking liquid. Add 1/4 teaspoon finely chopped saffron threads to the reserved hot cooking liquid and leave to stand for 1–2 minutes. Mash the drained potatoes, add 2 crushed garlic cloves, 20 g (1 tablespoon) chopped butter, 2 tablespoons cream, 1/4 teaspoon salt and the saffron liquid. Mix well with a wooden spoon and serve immediately. Serves 4–6.

SUGARSNAP PEAS WITH TOASTED ALMONDS AND PANCETTA

Heat 2 teaspoons olive oil in a large frying pan, add 1 small chopped onion and 2 finely chopped slices pancetta, and cook over a medium heat for 2 minutes. Add 300 g (10 1/2 oz) sugarsnap peas and stir-fry for 2–3 minutes, or until tender. Remove from the heat, add 40 g (1/3 cup) toasted slivered almonds and toss to coat. Season with salt and pepper and serve immediately. Serves 4–6.

Opposite page top to bottom:
Citrus-glazed carrots, Roasted tomatoes with balsamic and basil, Baked sweet potato chips.
This page top to bottom:
Mixed steamed Asian greens, Saffron mashed potato, Sugarsnap peas with toasted almonds and pancetta.

SNAPPER FILLETS WITH TOMATO JAM ON WHITE BEAN SKORDALIA

Skordalia is a traditional Greek sauce flavoured with garlic, ground almonds and lemon juice or vinegar and thickened with bread. There are many regional variations on this classic sauce.

Preparation time: 20 minutes
Total cooking time: 45 minutes

TOMATO JAM
1 tablespoon olive oil
1 small onion, finely chopped
2 garlic cloves, crushed
1 teaspoon yellow mustard seeds
400 g (14 oz) Roma (plum) tomatoes,
    chopped
1½ tablespoons caster
    (superfine) sugar
80 ml (⅓ cup) sherry
2 teaspoons red wine vinegar
2 teaspoons finely chopped oregano

SKORDALIA
2 x 400 g (14 oz) tins cannellini
    beans, rinsed and drained
95 g (½ cup) ground almonds
1 tablespoon lemon juice
3 garlic cloves, chopped
125 ml (½ cup) olive oil
1 teaspoon finely chopped oregano

SNAPPER FILLETS
1 tablespoon olive oil, for pan-frying
4 x 150–200 g (5½–6 oz) pieces
    snapper fillet, skin on
black olives, to garnish
oregano, to garnish
extra virgin olive oil, to serve

1 To make the jam, heat the oil in a saucepan over a medium heat. Cook the onion for 5 minutes, or until lightly browned, then add the garlic and mustard and stir for 1 minute, or until fragrant. Add the tomato, sugar, sherry, vinegar, oregano, 2 tablespoons water and some salt. Reduce to a simmer and cook, stirring often, for 30 minutes, or until pulpy. Remove from the heat, cover and keep warm.

2 Meanwhile, to make the skordalia, put the beans, almonds, lemon juice and garlic in a food processor and process until smooth. While the motor is running, gradually add the oil and process until thick and creamy. Transfer to a saucepan over low heat and stir until heated through. Season, cover and keep warm.

3 Heat the oil in a large frying pan over a medium heat. Sprinkle the skin of the snapper with some salt, then add to the pan, skin-side-down and cook for 2–3 minutes each side.

4 To serve, stir the oregano through the skordalia, place a large spoonful on each plate, top with the snapper and a dollop of the jam. Garnish with olives and oregano and drizzle a little extra virgin olive oil around the plate.

LAMB WITH SPICY LENTILS
AND RAITA

SERVES 4

Backstraps or loin fillets can be used here, depending on what looks good at the butcher shop.

Preparation time: 30 minutes + 30 minutes standing
Total cooking time: 1 hour

SPICY LENTILS
2 tablespoons olive oil
1 onion, chopped
1 carrot, diced
3 garlic cloves, finely chopped
2 teaspoons ground coriander
  (cilantro)
½ teaspoon ground cinnamon
½ teaspoon ground cloves
1 teaspoon ground turmeric
2 teaspoons ground cumin
½ teaspoon cayenne pepper
1 large tomato, diced
185 g (1 cup) brown lentils, washed
coriander (cilantro) leaves, to garnish

RAITA
1 small cucumber, grated
250 g (1 cup) plain yoghurt
½ small red onion, finely chopped
1 garlic clove, crushed
3 tablespoons coriander (cilantro)
  leaves, chopped
1 tablespoon lemon juice
½ teaspoon ground cumin
pinch cayenne pepper

LAMB
1 small cinnamon stick
2 teaspoons cardamom seeds
2 cloves
2 teaspoons cumin seeds
½ teaspoon chilli flakes
1 tablespoon coriander (cilantro)
  seeds
2 x 250 g (9 oz) lamb backstraps
  or loin fillets
1 tablespoon olive oil

1 To make the spicy lentils, heat the oil in a large saucepan, add the onion and carrot and cook, stirring, for 7 minutes, or until the onion is soft. Stir in the garlic and cook for 2–3 minutes, then add the spices and stir for 1 minute, or until fragrant. Add the tomato, lentils, 1 teaspoon salt and 1 litre (4 cups) of water. Bring to the boil, then reduce the heat and simmer for 30–40 minutes, or until the lentils are soft and most of the liquid is absorbed. Add more water if it is too dry. Season.

2 Meanwhile, to prepare the raita, toss the cucumber with 1 teaspoon of salt and drain in a colander for 30 minutes. Rinse, then squeeze the cucumber to remove any excess liquid and combine with the remaining ingredients. Leave until ready to use.

3 Preheat the oven to 240°C (475°F/Gas 9). Preheat a baking tray. Combine the spices for the lamb in a dry frying pan and toast, shaking the pan frequently, over a medium heat for 2 minutes, or until smoking and fragrant. Grind the spices together coarsely. Season the lamb, then rub on the spice blend.

4 Heat a large frying pan over a medium heat. Add the oil, then the lamb and brown each side for 2 minutes. Transfer to the hot baking tray and roast for 3–5 minutes, or until cooked to your liking. Remove from the oven, cover with foil and rest for 5–10 minutes. Cut the meat across the grain into thin slices.

5 Put a heap of lentils in the centre of each plate. Arrange 6–8 lamb pieces around the lentils, then add a dollop of raita. Garnish with coriander.

BLUE-EYE COD WITH SALSA VERDE POTATOES

SERVES 4

The tasty combination of ingredients that make up salsa verde, or green sauce, also complement cold meats, salads and hard-boiled eggs.

Preparation time: 20 minutes
Total cooking time: 25 minutes

115 g (2 large handfuls) English
   spinach leaves, blanched and
   squeezed dry
2 tablespoons chopped flat-leaf
   (Italian) parsley
2 tablespoons snipped chives
1 tablespoon drained capers
2 anchovy fillets
1 hard-boiled egg, chopped
1 tablespoon white wine vinegar
60 ml (1/4 cup) extra virgin olive oil
500 g (1 lb 2 oz) pink eye or
   desiree potatoes
oil, for pan-frying
4 x 150 g (5½ oz) blue-eye cod
   or other firm white fish fillets
125 g (4½ oz) butter
3 garlic cloves, finely chopped
1 tablespoon lime juice
1½ tablespoons lime zest

1 To make the salsa verde, put the spinach, parsley, chives, capers, anchovy fillets, egg and vinegar in a food processor and process until combined. With the motor running, gradually add the extra virgin olive oil in a thin, steady stream and process until smooth.

2 Cook the potatoes in a large saucepan of boiling water for about 18 minutes, or until tender. Drain and cool slightly, then cut into 1 cm (1/2 in) slices. Carefully fold the salsa verde through the warm potatoes.

3 Meanwhile, heat the oil in a frying pan over a medium heat and cook the fish in batches for 3–5 minutes each side, or until tender. Remove from the pan and keep warm.

4 Reduce the heat slightly, add the butter and cook until just brown, then stir in the garlic and lime juice.

5 Serve the blue-eye cod on a bed of potatoes, then drizzle with the butter and top with lime zest.

THAI-SPICED PORK WITH GREEN MANGO SALAD

SERVES 4 AS A MAIN (6 AS A STARTER)

Green mango has a slightly sour taste that is popular in salads, pickles and chutneys across Asia.

Preparation time: 45 minutes + 2 hours refrigeration
Total cooking time: 10 minutes

2 stalks lemon grass (white part
   only), thinly sliced
1 garlic clove
2 red Asian shallots
1 tablespoon coarsely chopped
   fresh ginger
1 red bird's-eye chilli, seeded
1 tablespoon fish sauce
1 small handful coriander (cilantro)
1 teaspoon grated lime zest
1 tablespoon lime juice
2 tablespoons oil
2 pork tenderloins, trimmed
steamed jasmine rice (optional)

DRESSING
1 large red chilli, seeded and
   finely chopped
2 garlic cloves, finely chopped
3 coriander (cilantro) roots,
   finely chopped
1¼ tablespoons grated palm sugar
2 tablespoons fish sauce
60 ml (¼ cup) lime juice

SALAD
2 green mangoes or 1 small green
   papaya, peeled, pitted and cut
   into julienne strips
1 carrot, grated
45 g (½ cup) bean sprouts
½ red onion, thinly sliced
3 tablespoons roughly chopped mint
3 tablespoons roughly chopped
   coriander (cilantro) leaves
3 tablespoons roughly chopped
   Vietnamese mint

1 Put the lemon grass, garlic, shallots, ginger, chilli, fish sauce, coriander, lime zest, lime juice and oil in a blender or food processor and process until a coarse paste forms. Transfer to a non-metallic dish. Coat the pork in the marinade, then cover and refrigerate for at least 2 hours, but no longer than 4 hours.

2 To make the salad dressing, mix all the ingredients together in a bowl.

3 Combine all the salad ingredients in a large bowl.

4 Preheat a grill or chargrill pan and cook the pork over a medium heat for 4–5 minutes each side, or until cooked through. Remove from the heat, rest for 5 minutes, then slice.

5 Toss the dressing and salad together. Season to taste with salt and cracked black pepper. Arrange the sliced pork in a circle in the centre of each plate and top with salad. To make this a main course, serve with steamed jasmine rice, if desired.

BEEF RIB ROAST WITH
GARLIC BREAD AND BUTTER PUDDINGS

SERVES 4

These individual puddings are a delicious alternative to Yorkshire puddings and very simple to make. You could cook one large pudding, if you prefer.

Preparation time: 35 minutes + 35 minutes standing
Total cooking time: 2 hours

BEETROOT RELISH
3 baby beetroot
1 teaspoon sea salt flakes
1 tablespoon olive oil
2–3 teaspoons horseradish cream
2 gherkins, finely chopped
1 garlic clove, crushed
2 teaspoons red wine vinegar
2 teaspoons whole-egg mayonnaise
2 tablespoons finely chopped
    flat-leaf (Italian) parsley

RIB ROAST
1.6 kg (3 lb 8 oz) beef standing rib
    roast (4 racks), very well trimmed
2 tablespoons olive oil
1 tablespoon plain (all-purpose) flour
250 ml (1 cup) red wine
250 ml (1 cup) beef stock
1 tablespoon green peppercorns

GARLIC BREAD AND BUTTER
    PUDDINGS
60 ml (¼ cup) milk
125 ml (½ cup) cream
10 garlic cloves, chopped
1 egg
1 tablespoon finely chopped
    flat-leaf (Italian) parsley
softened butter, to spread
6 slices white bread

1 Preheat the oven to 200°C (400°F/Gas 6). To make the beetroot relish, trim the beetroot and cut them into halves. Toss with the salt and oil in a roasting tin and cook for 40–45 minutes, or until tender when tested with the point of a knife. Remove from the oven and cover with foil until cool enough to handle. Reduce the oven to 190°C (375°F/Gas 5).

2 Peel and coarsely grate the beetroot, then place in a bowl with the horseradish, gherkin, garlic, vinegar, mayonnaise and parsley, then mix well and season. Cover and set aside.

3 Season the beef well. Pour the oil into a large heavy-based frying pan over a high heat, then sear the beef for 2 minutes each side, or until well browned. Transfer the beef to a roasting tin, setting the frying pan aside to use for the sauce. Roast the beef for 1 hour until medium-rare, or until cooked to your liking. (The cooking time will vary depending on the size of the roast.) Remove from the oven and rest for 20 minutes. Leave the oven on.

4 Meanwhile, to make the puddings, combine the milk, cream and garlic in a saucepan and bring to the boil, then reduce the heat and simmer for 10 minutes. Remove from the heat and leave to infuse for 15 minutes. Strain the mixture into a jug. Whisk in the egg and extra parsley and season.

5 Lightly butter the bread on both sides, then remove the crusts and cut the bread into 1.5 cm (½ in) squares. Press the bread into four 125 ml (½ cup) muffin holes and gradually pour the custard over them, allowing the bread to absorb the custard before each addition. Leave for 15 minutes.

6 While the meat is resting, put the bread and butter puddings in the oven and cook for 12 minutes, or until puffed and golden. Remove from the muffin holes—you may need to loosen them with a knife.

7 Meanwhile, reheat the frying pan in which the beef was cooked. Sprinkle the pan with flour and stir over a medium heat for 1 minute, then add the wine and stock. Scrape up any sediment and cook for 6–8 minutes, or until thickened slightly. Stir in the green peppercorns. Season well and remove from the heat, then cover and set aside.

8 Add any juices from the rested meat to the sauce and reheat gently. Cut down between the racks of beef, dividing into four even pieces. Arrange on a plate with the pudding and a little beetroot relish, then drizzle the peppercorn sauce over the meat and around the plate.

SEAFOOD RISOTTO

SERVES 4 (6 AS A STARTER)

Rice and seafood is a superb combination and one that's easy to adapt. Paella—the popular Spanish favourite—throws together a variety of meat, vegetables and seafood to great effect.

Preparation time: 30 minutes
Total cooking time: 40 minutes

12 baby clams or pipis
375 ml (1½ cups) white wine
875 ml (3½ cups) vegetable stock
2 bay leaves
1 celery stalk, chopped
6 French shallots, chopped
60 ml (¼ cup) lemon juice
12 raw king prawns (shrimps),
    peeled and deveined
12 scallops, cleaned and roes
    removed
1 squid tube, cut into 12 slices
1 tablespoon olive oil
2 tablespoons butter
80 g (⅔ cup) chopped spring
    onions (scallions)
4–6 garlic cloves, crushed
1½ tablespoons finely
    chopped thyme
330 g (1½ cups) calasparra or
    risotto rice
90 g (⅓ cup) sour cream
35 g (⅓ cup) grated Parmesan
    cheese
2 tablespoons chopped
    flat-leaf (Italian) parsley
shaved Parmesan cheese, to serve

1 Scrub and rinse the clams to remove any grit, discarding any that are opened or damaged. Put the wine, stock, bay leaves, celery, shallots, lemon juice and 625 ml (2½ cups) of water in a saucepan and bring to the boil for 5 minutes. Reduce the heat to a simmer, then add the clams and cook for 3 minutes, or until they open. Using a slotted spoon, transfer the clams to a bowl, discarding any that did not open. Add the prawns to the stock and cook for 2 minutes, or until pink and curled, then transfer to the bowl with the clams. Add the scallops and squid tubes and cook for 1 minute, then transfer to the bowl. Strain the stock, then return to the pan and keep at a low simmer.

2 Heat the oil and half the butter in a large heavy-based saucepan over a medium heat. Add the spring onion, garlic and thyme and cook, stirring, for 1 minute. Stir in the rice and cook for 1 minute, or until well coated.

3 Add 125 ml (½ cup) of the hot stock. Stir constantly over a medium heat until all the stock is absorbed. Continue adding more stock, 125 ml (½ cup) at a time, stirring constantly for 25 minutes, or until the stock is absorbed. Add the seafood with the final addition of stock. The rice should be tender and creamy.

4 Remove from the heat and stir in the sour cream, Parmesan cheese and parsley. Season. Serve with shaved Parmesan cheese.

TERIYAKI PORK WITH SOYA BEANS

SERVES 4

The term teriyaki is a Japanese compound word formed from 'teri', referring to the gloss of the soy sauce and rice wine marinade, and yaki 'grill'.

Preparation time: 20 minutes + 2 hours refrigeration + 10 minutes resting
Total cooking time: 30 minutes

1½ tablespoons soy sauce
5 teaspoons grated ginger
2 garlic cloves, crushed
60 ml (¼ cup) oil
60 ml (¼ cup) dry sherry
700 g (1 lb 9 oz) pork fillet
2 tablespoons honey
300 g (10½ oz) frozen soya beans
4 baby bok choy (pak choi), sliced
   in half lengthways
3 teaspoons sesame oil
sesame seeds, toasted, to garnish
   (optional)

1 Put the soy sauce, 3 teaspoons of the ginger, 1 clove of garlic and 2 tablespoons each of the oil and sherry in a large shallow non-metallic dish and mix well. Add the pork and toss gently to coat well. Cover and refrigerate for 2 hours, turning the meat occasionally. Preheat the oven to 180°C (350°F/Gas 4).

2 Remove the pork and drain well, reserving the marinade. Pat the pork dry with paper towels. Heat the remaining oil in a large frying pan and cook the pork over a medium heat for 5–6 minutes, or until browned all over. Transfer to a baking tray and roast for 10–15 minutes. Cover with foil and rest for 10 minutes.

3 Put the reserved marinade, honey, the remaining sherry and ⅓ cup (80 ml) water in a small saucepan and bring to the boil. Reduce the heat and simmer for 3–4 minutes, or until reduced to a glaze. Keep the glaze hot.

4 Cook the soya beans in a large covered saucepan of lightly salted boiling water for 1 minute, then add the bok choy and cook for a further 2 minutes. Drain. Heat the sesame oil in the same saucepan, add the remaining ginger and garlic and heat for 30 seconds. Return the soya beans and bok choy to the pan and toss gently.

5 Slice the pork. Put the vegetables on a large serving dish and top with the pork slices. Spoon the glaze over the pork, sprinkle with sesame seeds and serve immediately.

CARAMELIZED APPLE MOUSSE

SERVES 4

You can cook with most sorts of apples, but green apples are very juicy, something that is particularly suitable for this mousse. Any tartness will be counterbalanced by the caramel.

Preparation time: 20 minutes + 3 hours refrigeration
Total cooking time: 20 minutes

50 g (2½ tablespoons) unsalted
   butter
60 g (¼ cup) caster (superfine)
   sugar
170 ml (⅔ cup) cream
500 g (1 lb 2 oz) green apples,
   peeled, cored and cut into
   thin wedges
2 eggs, separated

1 Put the butter and sugar in a frying pan and stir over a low heat until the sugar has dissolved. Increase the heat to medium and cook until the mixture turns deeply golden, stirring frequently. Add 2 tablespoons of the cream and stir to remelt the caramel.

2 Add the apple wedges and cook, stirring frequently, over a medium heat for 10–15 minutes, or until caramelized. Remove eight apple wedges and set aside to use as a garnish.

3 Blend the remaining apples and caramel in a food processor until smooth. Transfer to a large bowl, then stir in the egg yolks and leave to cool.

4 Whisk the egg whites in a clean, dry bowl until soft peaks form, then fold into the cooled apple mixture.

5 Whip the remaining cream until firm peaks form and fold into the apple mixture. Pour into a 750 ml (3 cup) serving bowl or four 185 ml (¾ cup) individual serving moulds. Refrigerate for 3 hours, or until firm. Serve with the reserved apple wedges.

DARK CHOCOLATE ICE CREAM
WITH HAZELNUT MERINGUES

SERVES 6

You can use ordinary ramekins or dariole moulds—small bucket-shaped moulds—if you have them.

Preparation time: 35 minutes + cooling time + 6 hours freezing
Total cooking time: 1 hour 30 minutes

8 egg yolks
125 g (1/2 cup) caster (superfine)
    sugar
40 g (1/3 cup) malted milk powder
500 ml (2 cups) cream
250 ml (1 cup) milk
1 vanilla bean, split lengthways
100 g (31/2 oz) dark chocolate,
    melted

MERINGUES
3 egg whites
170 g (6 oz) caster (superfine)
    sugar
1/4 teaspoon vanilla essence
60 g (1/2 cup) toasted, skinned
    and finely chopped hazelnuts

1 Put the egg yolks in a large non-metallic bowl and gradually whisk in the sugar with a whisk until the sugar has dissolved and the mixture is thick and pale. (Do not use electric beaters or they will incorporate too much air.)

2 Divide the mixture into two smaller bowls and add the malt to one.

3 Combine the cream and milk in a saucepan. Scrape the seeds from the vanilla bean into the pan and add the pod. Slowly bring to the boil over a medium heat. Remove the pod, then whisk half the mixture into each bowl.

4 Transfer all of the malt-flavoured custard to a small, clean saucepan and cook over a low heat, stirring constantly, for about 20 minutes, or until thick and it coats the back of a spoon. Remove from the heat, strain into a bowl, cover with plastic wrap and cool completely. Repeat with the plain custard, stirring the melted chocolate into the strained mixture.

5 Pour the cooled malt custard into a shallow metal tin, cover with plastic wrap and freeze for 2 hours, or until almost set. Scoop into a chilled bowl and beat with electric beaters until smooth. Return to the tin and refreeze for 1 hour. Repeat this process twice or freeze in an ice-cream maker according to the manufacturer's instructions, until frozen but still spreadable. Smooth the malt ice cream into the base of six 170 ml (2/3 cup) dariole moulds or ramekins and freeze. Repeat the freezing and churning process with the chocolate custard, then spread over the frozen malt ice cream. Freeze until completely frozen.

6 To make the meringues, preheat the oven to 140°C (275°F/ Gas 1). Put the egg whites in a large clean, dry bowl and whisk until stiff. Gradually add the sugar, whisking well after each addition until stiff and glossy; add the vanilla essence with the final portion of sugar.

7 Gently fold the hazelnuts into the meringue mixture, then spoon into a piping bag with a 1 cm (1/2 in) plain nozzle. Line a baking tray with baking paper and pipe six large meringue spirals onto the paper, starting from the centre and working out. Bake the meringues for 1 hour, or until dry. Cool on a wire rack. Store in an airtight container. To serve, briefly dip the bases of the ice cream moulds into warm water, run a flat-bladed knife around the inside edge and unmould onto a large plate. Top with the meringues.

145

FLOURLESS CHOCOLATE CAKE

SERVES 10

News from the science lab just keeps getting sweeter—not only does chocolate release endorphins that make us feel good, it also contains enzymes with a variety of health benefits.

Preparation time: 1 hour + overnight refrigeration + 40 minutes standing
Total cooking time: 1 hour 15 minutes

500 g (1 lb 2 oz) good-quality dark
    chocolate, chopped
6 eggs
2 tablespoons Frangelico or brandy
165 g (1½ cups) ground hazelnuts
250 ml (1 cup) cream, whipped
icing (confectioners') sugar, to dust
thick (double/heavy) cream,
    to serve (optional)

1 Preheat the oven to 150°C (300°F/Gas 2). Grease a deep 20 cm (8 in) round cake tin and line the base with baking paper.

2 Put the chocolate in a heatproof bowl. Half-fill a saucepan with water and bring to the boil. Remove from the heat and sit the bowl over the pan, making sure it is not touching the water. Stir occasionally until the chocolate has melted.

3 Put the eggs in a large heatproof bowl and add the Frangelico. Put the bowl over a saucepan of barely simmering water on a low heat, making sure the bowl does not touch the water. Beat the mixture with electric beaters on a high speed for 7 minutes, or until light and foamy. Remove from the heat.

4 Using a metal spoon, quickly and lightly fold the melted chocolate and ground nuts into the egg mixture until just combined. Fold in the cream and pour into the prepared tin. Put the cake tin in a shallow roasting tin. Pour enough hot water into the roasting tin to come halfway up the side of the cake tin.

5 Bake the cake for 1 hour, or until just set. Remove the cake tin from the roasting tin and cool to room temperature. Cover with plastic wrap and refrigerate overnight.

6 Invert the cake onto a plate and remove the baking paper. Cut into slices, dust lightly with icing sugar and serve with thick cream.

PEARS IN SPICED WINE JELLY
WITH FROZEN CARDAMOM PARFAIT

SERVES 6

If you can't find small pears, use regular-sized ones and pare them down to fit into the mould.

Preparation time: 50 minutes + 1 hour 20 minutes cooling + overnight freezing
Total cooking time: 40 minutes

CARDAMOM PARFAIT
185 ml (3/4 cup) milk
1/4 teaspoon cardamom seeds
4 egg yolks
125 g (1/2 cup) caster (superfine)
    sugar
250 ml (1 cup) cream

PEARS IN SPICED WINE JELLY
6 x 90 g (31/4 oz) corella pears or
    other small pears
250 ml (1 cup) red wine
1 cinnamon stick, broken
3 whole cloves
pinch cardamom seeds
125 g (1/2 cup) caster (superfine)
    sugar
2 teaspoons gelatine

1 Lightly oil a 24 x 7 cm (9 x 2 1/2 in) bar tin, then line the base and long sides with plastic wrap, allowing the excess to hang over the edges. Put the milk and cardamom seeds in a saucepan, bring to the boil, then remove from the heat, cover and infuse for 10 minutes. Strain the mixture into a jug.

2 Beat the egg yolks and sugar in a small bowl with electric beaters until thick and pale, then gradually beat in the warm milk. Return the mixture to the saucepan and stir over a medium heat for about 5 minutes, or until the mixture thickens slightly. Remove from the heat and pour into a bowl. Cover with plastic wrap, then refrigerate until cold.

3 Beat the cream in a bowl until soft peaks form, then gently fold into the cold custard mixture until combined. Pour into the prepared tin and fold the plastic gently over the top. Freeze overnight, or until firm.

4 Peel the pears, leaving the stems attached, then remove the core from the bottom with a melon baller. Check that the pears will fit in 125 ml (1/2 cup) dariole moulds or ramekins. If the pears are too large, use a vegetable peeler to slice off some of the pear until it just fits—but go slowly so that you don't cut off too much. Trim the bases so that the pears will sit flat.

5 Put the wine, cinnamon, cloves, cardamom seeds, sugar and 185 ml (3/4 cup) of water in a saucepan large enough for the pears. Stir over a medium heat until the sugar dissolves. Add the pears, cover and simmer for about 30 minutes, or until soft. Remove the pan from the heat and allow to cool.

6 Drain the pears well, reserving 250 ml (1 cup) of the liquid—if there is not enough, add water to make up the difference. Put the pears in the moulds.

7 Pour 60 ml (1/4 cup) of the liquid into a bowl and sprinkle the gelatine over it evenly. Leave until the gelatine is spongy: do not stir. Bring a small saucepan of water to the boil, remove from the heat and put the bowl with the gelatine mixture in the saucepan so the water comes halfway up the side of the bowl. Stir the gelatine until it dissolves, then pour it into the remaining poaching liquid and stir together. Refrigerate, stirring occasionally, for 20 minutes until the mixture has a jelly-like consistency.

8 Pour the mixture into the dariole moulds around the pears, standing the pears up if they fall over. Refrigerate for 1 hour, or until set.

9 Briefly dip the moulds in warm water and remove the pears. Put on serving plates. Remove the parfait from the tin, unwrap, then cut into eight slices. Put two slices next to each of the pears. Serve immediately.

CITRUS TART

SERVES 6–8

Citrus fruits have a refreshing and cleansing flavour that is always welcome at the end of a meal and is particularly good during the warmer months of the year.

Preparation time: 1 hour + 30 minutes refrigeration
Total cooking time: 1 hour 45 minutes

PASTRY
125 g (1 cup) plain (all-purpose) flour
75 g (2½ oz) unsalted butter,
    softened
1 egg yolk
2 tablespoons icing (confectioners')
    sugar, sifted

FILLING
3 eggs
2 egg yolks
185 g (¾ cup) caster (superfine)
    sugar
125 ml (½ cup) cream
185 ml (¾ cup) lemon juice
1½ tablespoons finely grated lemon
    zest
2 small lemons
160 g (⅔ cup) sugar

1 To make the pastry, sift the flour and a pinch of salt into a large bowl. Make a well in the centre and add the butter, egg yolk and icing sugar. Work together the butter, yolk and sugar with your fingertips, then slowly incorporate the flour. Bring together into a ball—you may need to add a few drops of cold water. Flatten the ball slightly, cover with plastic wrap and refrigerate for 20 minutes.

2 Preheat the oven to 200°C (400°F/Gas 6). Lightly grease a shallow 21 cm (8 in) loose-bottomed flan tin.

3 Roll the pastry out between two sheets of baking paper to an even thickness to fit the base and side of the tin. Trim the edge. Chill for 10 minutes. Line the pastry with crumpled baking paper, fill with baking beads or rice and bake for 10 minutes, or until cooked. Remove the paper and beads and bake for 6–8 minutes, or until the pastry looks dry all over. Cool the pastry and reduce the oven to 150°C (300°F/Gas 2).

4 Whisk the eggs, yolks and sugar together, add the cream and juice and mix well. Strain into a jug and add the zest. Put the flan tin on a baking sheet on the middle shelf of the oven and carefully pour in the filling. Bake for 40 minutes, or until just set—it should wobble in the middle when the tin is firmly tapped. Cool before removing from the tin.

5 Wash and scrub the lemons well. Slice very thinly. Combine the sugar and 200 ml of water in a small frying pan and stir over a low heat until the sugar has dissolved. Add the lemon slices and simmer over a low heat for 40 minutes, or until the peel is very tender and the pith looks transparent. Lift out of the syrup and drain on baking paper. If serving the tart immediately, cover the surface with the lemon slices. If not, keep the slices covered and decorate the tart when ready to serve. Serve with whipped cream, if desired.

PASSIONFRUIT CUSTARD WITH LEMON LANGUES DES CHATS

SERVES 4

The evocatively named langue de chat, or 'cat's tongue', is a flat, thin sweet biscuit with rounded ends that is usually accompanied by dessert wine.

Preparation time: 25 minutes + 1 hour 30 minutes cooling time
Total cooking time: 40 minutes

4 egg yolks
60 g (1/4 cup) caster (superfine)
    sugar
75 ml (1/3 cup) milk
75 ml (1/3 cup) cream
Seedless pulp from 1 passionfruit
50 ml (3 tablespoons) lemon juice
icing (confectioners') sugar, to dust

LEMON LANGUES DES CHATS
60 g (2¼ oz) unsalted butter,
    softened slightly
125 g (1/2 cup) caster (superfine)
    sugar
1/2 teaspoon finely grated lemon
    zest
2 egg whites
50 g (1¾ oz) plain (all-purpose)
    flour

1 Preheat the oven to 140°C (275°F/Gas 1). To make the custard, beat the egg yolks and sugar together, then mix in the milk, followed by the cream and finally the passionfruit pulp and lemon juice.

2 Divide the mixture among four 125 ml (1/2 cup) ramekins. Put the ramekins in a roasting tin and pour in enough warm water to come halfway up the side of the ramekins. Put the roasting tin in the oven and cook the custards for 30 minutes, or until set. Remove the ramekins from the water bath and cool on a wire rack before transferring them to the refrigerator. Refrigerate for at least 1 hour. Increase the oven to 190°C (375°F/Gas 5).

3 Lightly grease two baking trays. To make the langues des chats, put the butter, sugar and lemon zest in a small bowl and beat together with a wooden spoon until pale and creamy. Add the egg whites and beat briefly. Sift the flour into the mixture and fold it in.

4 Transfer the mixture to a piping bag with a 1 cm (1/2 in) wide, plain nozzle. Pipe the mixture into 8 cm (3 in) long strips on the baking trays, squeezing a little harder at each end to achieve the 'cat's tongue' shape and spacing them well apart to allow for spreading. Cook in the preheated oven for 5–7 minutes, or until the edges and base of the biscuits are lightly brown.

5 Remove the biscuits from the oven. After a couple of minutes, transfer the biscuits to a wire rack and cool completely. Dust the custards with a little icing sugar and serve each with two langues des chats.

RASPBERRY BAVAROIS WITH BERRY SAUCE

SERVES 4

It's fine to change the berry combinations in the bavarois and accompanying sauce. You can also use frozen berries in place of fresh, perhaps with a dash of Cointreau.

Preparation time: 20 minutes + cooling time + 3 hours refrigeration
Total cooking time: 15 minutes

125 ml (1/2 cup) cream
200 g (7 oz) raspberries
2 tablespoons raspberry liqueur
2 teaspoons lemon juice
90 g (1/3 cup) caster (superfine)
    sugar
1 egg, separated
125 ml (1/2 cup) milk
1/2 teaspoon vanilla essence
3 teaspoons gelatine
1 tablespoon unsalted butter
2 tablespoons soft brown sugar
250 g (9 oz) strawberries, halved
150 g (51/2 oz) blueberries

1 Pour the cream into a bowl and beat until firm peaks form, then cover and refrigerate until needed. Process the raspberries, 1 tablespoon of the liqueur, 1 teaspoon of the lemon juice and 60 g (1/4 cup) of the caster sugar in a food processor until smooth. Strain through a sieve.

2 Put the egg yolk and remaining sugar in a bowl and whisk until pale and thickened, then whisk in the milk. Put the bowl on top of a small saucepan of simmering water and stir continuously for 5–10 minutes, or until the custard thickens slightly and coats the back of a spoon. Add the vanilla and remove from the heat.

3 Stir the gelatine into 1 tablespoon of hot water until dissolved, then stir into the custard. Cool to room temperature, then add the berry purée.

4 Whisk the egg white and a pinch of sugar together until firm peaks form, fold into the berry mixture, then slowly fold in the cream. Pour into four lightly oiled 185 ml (3/4 cup) moulds. Chill for 3 hours, or until set.

5 To make the sauce, combine the butter, brown sugar, remaining liqueur and lemon juice and 1 tablespoon water in a large frying pan, bring to the boil and cook for 1–2 minutes, or until thickened slightly. Add the berries and stir for 1–2 minutes, or until heated through, then remove from the heat and cool slightly.

6 Unmould the bavarois by running a knife around the edge, then turn out onto a plate. Spoon the sauce around the bavarois and serve.

BANANA TEMPURA WITH
GREEN TEA ICE CREAM

SERVES 4

The Japanese cooking style known as tempura need not be limited to seafood, vegetables and other savoury dishes—it's equally good used with a variety of fruits.

Preparation time: 30 minutes + overnight refrigeration
Total cooking time: 25 minutes

ICE CREAM
10 g (1/3 cup) Japanese green
    tea leaves
500 ml (2 cups) milk
6 egg yolks
125 g (1/2 cup) caster (superfine)
    sugar
500 ml (2 cups) cream

BANANA TEMPURA
oil, for deep-frying
1 egg
185 ml (3/4 cup) iced water
85 g (2/3 cup) tempura flour
4 small bananas, split in half
    lengthways and cut in half
    crossways
caster (superfine) sugar, to sprinkle
warmed honey, to serve (optional)

1 Combine the tea leaves and the milk in a saucepan and bring to simmering point over a low heat. Do not rush this step—the longer the milk takes to come to a simmer, the better the flavour. Set aside for 5 minutes before straining the liquid into a bowl.

2 Whisk the egg yolks and sugar in a heatproof bowl until thick and pale, then add the infused milk. Put the bowl over a saucepan of simmering water, making sure that the base of the bowl is not touching the water. Stir the custard until it is thick enough to coat the back of spoon, then remove from the heat and allow to cool slightly before adding the cream.

3 Pour the mixture into a metal tray and freeze for 1 1/2–2 hours, or until just frozen around the edges. Transfer the mixture to a chilled bowl, beat with electric beaters until thick and creamy, then return to the metal tray. Repeat the freezing and beating twice more. Transfer to a storage container, cover the surface with baking paper and freeze overnight. Alternatively, freeze in an ice-cream maker according to the manufacturer's instructions.

4 Heat the oil in a deep-fryer or heavy-based saucepan until a cube of bread browns in 20 seconds. Mix together the egg and water in a bowl, then stir in the tempura flour. Do not whisk the batter—it must be lumpy.

5 Dip the banana quarters into the batter and deep-fry a few at a time for about 2 minutes, or until crisp and golden. Drain on paper towels and sprinkle with caster sugar. Serve four pieces of banana with a scoop of ice cream. Drizzle with warmed honey.

FROZEN ZABAGLIONE WITH MARSALA SAUCE

SERVES 4

The sweet overtones of Marsala give this creamy Italian dessert a fabulous velvety richness. Serve it with a glass on the side, if you desire.

Preparation time: 15 minutes + 6 hours freezing
Total cooking time: 10 minutes

170 ml (2/3 cup) cream
3 egg yolks
1/2 teaspoon vanilla essence
185 ml (3/4 cup) Marsala
90 g (1/3 cup) caster (superfine) sugar
50 g (1/3 cup) whole blanched
   almonds, toasted and chopped

1 Whip the cream to firm peaks, then cover and refrigerate until needed.

2 Put the egg yolks, vanilla, 125 ml (1/2 cup) of the Marsala and half of the sugar in a non-metallic bowl and whisk well.

3 Fill one-third of a saucepan with water and bring to a simmer over a medium heat. Sit the bowl on top of the saucepan, making sure the base of the bowl does not touch the water. Whisk continuously for 5 minutes, or until thick and foamy. The mixture should hold its form when you drizzle some from the whisk.

4 Remove from the heat and stand in a bowl of ice, whisking for 3 minutes, or until cool. Remove from the ice, then gently fold in the whipped cream and almonds. Carefully pour into four 125 ml (1/2 cup) dariole moulds or ramekins, cover with plastic wrap and freeze for 6 hours, or until firm.

5 Combine the remaining Marsala and sugar in a small saucepan and stir over a low heat until the sugar dissolves. Bring just to the boil, then reduce the heat and simmer for 4–5 minutes, or until just syrupy—do not overcook or the syrup will harden when cool. Remove from the heat and set aside until needed.

6 Briefly dip the moulds into warm water, then loosen with a knife. Turn out onto a plate and drizzle with sauce. Garnish with almonds, if desired.

GRILLED FIGS WITH AMARETTO MASCARPONE

SERVES 4

Figs grilled with a little brown sugar and served with a dollop of yoghurt are an easy way to make yourself a treat, but for something extra special, serve them with mascarpone and vanilla caramel syrup.

Preparation time: 10 minutes
Total cooking time: 15 minutes

5½ tablespoons caster (superfine)
    sugar
60 ml (¼ cup) cream
½ teaspoon vanilla essence
110 g (½ cup) mascarpone cheese
2 tablespoons amaretto
35 g (¼ cup) blanched almonds,
    finely chopped
½ teaspoon ground cinnamon
6 fresh figs, halved

1 Line a baking tray with foil. Put three tablespoons of the caster sugar and 60 ml (¼ cup) of water in a small saucepan and stir over a low heat until the sugar has dissolved, brushing down the side of the pan with a clean brush dipped in water if any crystals appear. Bring to the boil and cook, without stirring, for about 8 minutes, swirling occasionally until the mixture is golden. Quickly remove the pan from the heat and carefully pour in the cream, stirring constantly until smooth, then stir in the vanilla.

2 To make the amaretto mascarpone, put the mascarpone, amaretto and 2 teaspoons of the remaining caster sugar in a bowl and mix together well.

3 Combine the chopped almonds, cinnamon and all the remaining caster sugar on a plate.

4 Press the cut side of each fig half into the almond mixture, then place, cut-side-up, onto the baking tray. Cook under a hot grill for 4–5 minutes, or until the sugar has caramelized and the almonds are toasted—watch them carefully to prevent burning.

5 Arrange three fig halves on each plate, place a dollop of the amaretto mascarpone to the side and drizzle with the sauce.

CROISSANT PUDDING WITH CHOCOLATE AND HAZELNUTS

SERVES 6–8

Bread and butter pudding is one of those comfort foods from childhood that never loses its appeal. This is an adult variation on that classic—rich, elegant and delectably more-ish.

Preparation time: 10 minutes + 10 minutes cooling
Total cooking time: 50 minutes

4 croissants, torn into pieces
100 g (3½ oz) dark chocolate, chopped into pieces
4 eggs
90 g (⅓ cup) caster (superfine) sugar
250 ml (1 cup) milk
250 ml (1 cup) cream
½ teaspoon grated orange zest
80 ml (⅓ cup) orange juice
2 tablespoons coarsely chopped hazelnuts

1 Preheat the oven to 180°C (350°F/Gas 4). Grease the base and sides of a 20 cm (8 in) deep-sided cake tin and line the tin with baking paper.
2 Place the croissant pieces in the tin, then scatter evenly with chocolate.
3 Beat the eggs and sugar together until pale and creamy.
4 Heat the milk and cream in a saucepan to almost boiling, then remove from the heat. Gradually pour into the egg mixture, stirring constantly. Add the orange zest and juice and stir well.
5 Slowly pour the mixture over the croissants, allowing the liquid to be absorbed before adding more. Sprinkle the top of the pudding with the hazelnuts and bake for 45 minutes, or until a skewer comes out clean when inserted in the centre.
6 Cool for 10 minutes. Run a knife around the edge, then turn out and invert. Cut into wedges and serve warm with cream, if desired.

WATERMELON GRANITA
WITH CITRUS VODKA

SERVES 4–6

Refresh your palate with the perfect summer thirst quencher. A tablespoon of finely chopped mint may be stirred through the mixture after you have strained the liquid.

Preparation time: 10 minutes + 5 hours freezing
Total cooking time: Nil

1 kg (2 lb 4 oz) piece of watermelon,
   rind removed to give 600 g
   (1 lb 5 oz) flesh
2 teaspoons lime juice
60 g (1/4 cup) caster (superfine)
   sugar
60 ml (1/4 cup) citrus-flavoured
   vodka

1 Coarsely chop the watermelon, removing the seeds. Put the flesh in a food processor and add the lime juice and sugar. Process until smooth, then strain through a fine sieve. Stir in the vodka, then taste—if the watermelon is not very sweet, you may have to add a little more sugar.
2 Pour into a shallow 1.5 litre (6 cup capacity) metal tin and freeze for about 1 hour, or until beginning to freeze around the edges. Scrape the frozen parts back into the mixture with a fork. Repeat every 30 minutes for about 4 hours, or until even-sized ice crystals have formed.
3 Serve immediately or beat with a fork just before serving. To serve, scrape into dishes with a fork.

ALMOND TUILES WITH CHERRY CONFIT AND ICE CREAM

SERVES 4

If you're feeling a little more ambitious, you could roll the tuiles up around a large metal horn mould, then fill them with ice cream and top with cherry confit.

Preparation time: 40 minutes + cooling time + 5 hours freezing
Total cooking time: 1 hour

ICE CREAM
300 g (10½ oz) sour cream
250 ml (1 cup) cream
1 vanilla bean, split lengthways
5 egg yolks
125 g (½ cup) caster (superfine) sugar

CHERRY CONFIT
3 x 425 g (15 oz) tins pitted black cherries
125 g (½ cup) caster (superfine) sugar
1 vanilla bean, split lengthways
1 cinnamon stick
2 star anise

ALMOND TUILES
2 egg whites
60 g (½ cup) icing (confectioners') sugar
60 g (½ cup) plain (all-purpose) flour, sifted
100 g (3½ oz) flaked almonds
40 g (1½ oz) unsalted butter, melted
¼ teaspoon ground cinnamon

1 To make the ice cream, place the sour cream, cream and vanilla bean in a saucepan and stir over a low heat until heated through.

2 Whisk the egg yolks and sugar in a bowl until pale and thick. Strain the cream mixture through a sieve into the egg mixture and whisk well. Return to a clean saucepan and stir constantly over a low heat for 5 minutes, or until it thickens slightly and coats the back of a spoon—do not boil or it will curdle. Pour into a bowl, cover with plastic wrap and cool.

3 When the mixture has cooled, pour it into a shallow metal tin, cover with plastic wrap and freeze for 2 hours, or until almost set. Scoop into a chilled bowl and beat with electric beaters until smooth. Return to the tin and refreeze for 1 hour. Repeat twice more or freeze in an ice-cream maker, according to the manufacturer's instructions.

4 To make the confit, drain the cherries, reserving 160 ml (⅔ cup) of the syrup. Place all the ingredients and reserved liquid in a saucepan and simmer, stirring occasionally, for 25 minutes, or until the sugar has dissolved and the confit is thick and syrupy. Remove from the heat. Cool.

5 Preheat the oven to 180°C (350°F/Gas 4). To make the tuiles, lightly grease two baking trays. Mark six 10 cm (4 in) circles on a sheet of baking paper big enough to fit a baking tray. Repeat with another sheet. Place the sheets, pencil-side-down, on the trays. Whisk the egg whites and icing sugar in a bowl until well combined. Mix in the flour, almonds, butter and cinnamon. Spread level tablespoons of the mixture onto the marked circles. Bake one tray at a time for 8–10 minutes, or until lightly golden around the edges. Cool for 30 seconds on the tray then transfer to a wire rack to cool.

6 To serve, place one tuile on each plate and top with a little of the confit. Repeat, then finish with a third tuile. Dust with icing sugar and serve with a scoop of the ice cream. Serve immediately.

WARM APPLE BAKLAVA WITH CINNAMON CREME ANGLAISE

SERVES 4

Baklava is a Turkish sweet consisting of chopped nuts between thin layers of filo pastry coated in syrup. This dessert combines the layering concept with the flavours of good old-fashioned apple pie.

Preparation time: 25 minutes
Total cooking time: 40 minutes

250 ml (1 cup) milk
2 cinnamon sticks
2 egg yolks
2 tablespoons caster (superfine)
  sugar
3 Granny Smith apples, peeled,
  cored and cut into small dice
1 tablespoon lemon juice
2 tablespoons unsalted butter
2 tablespoons honey
1/4 teaspoon allspice
1/4 teaspoon ground ginger
1 teaspoon rose-water
2 tablespoons chopped toasted
  almonds
2 tablespoons chopped walnuts
3 tablespoons pistachio nuts
2 sheets frozen puff pastry, thawed
1 tablespoon unsalted butter,
  melted
1 tablespoon icing sugar

1 Gently heat the milk and cinnamon sticks in a small saucepan and simmer for 5 minutes. Remove from the heat and infuse for about 5 minutes, then take out the cinnamon sticks.

2 Put the egg yolks and sugar in a small bowl and whisk well, then whisk in the milk until smooth. Transfer to a small saucepan and stir over a low heat for 10 minutes, or until the mixture is thick enough to coat the back of a spoon. Remove from the heat, cover and keep warm.

3 Preheat the oven to 200°C (400°F/Gas 6). Lightly grease two baking trays. Toss the apple in the lemon juice. Put the butter, honey, spices and rose-water in a frying pan and cook over a medium heat for 1 minute, or until the butter bubbles. Add the apple and cook, stirring occasionally, for 10 minutes, or until the apple begins to caramelize. Stir in the almonds, walnuts and 2 tablespoons of chopped pistachio nuts, then remove from the heat, cover and keep warm.

4 Lay the pastry sheets flat on a workbench, prick all over with a fork, then brush evenly with the melted butter. Sift the icing sugar over one of the sheets. Cut four 7 cm (2½ in) diamonds from each sheet, then carefully transfer to the baking trays. Bake for about 10 minutes, or until the pastry is crisp and golden. Reheat the apples gently if necessary.

5 To serve, divide the crème anglaise among four serving bowls and top with an unsugared pastry diamond. Divide the apple mixture among the pastry diamonds, then top with a sugared diamond. Garnish with 1 tablespoon of sliced pistachio nuts and serve.

172

STRAWBERRY TARTS WITH MASCARPONE CREAM

SERVES 6

Although strawberries are generally available all year, there's something decidedly summery about this tart. For best effect, serve it outdoors on a balmy evening.

Preparation time: 45 minutes + 45 minutes refrigeration
Total cooking time: 30 minutes

PASTRY
185 g (1¹/₂ cups) plain (all-purpose)
    flour
125 g unsalted butter, chilled and
    cut into cubes
80 ml (¹/₃ cup) iced water

FILLING
500 g (1 lb 2 oz) strawberries,
    hulled and halved
2 teaspoons vanilla essence
2 tablespoons Drambuie
60 g (¹/₃ cup) soft brown sugar
250 g (9 oz) mascarpone cheese
300 ml (1¹/₄ cups) thick
    (double/heavy) cream
2 teaspoons orange zest

1 Sift the flour into a large bowl and add the butter. Rub the butter into the flour with your fingertips until it resembles fine breadcrumbs. Make a well in the centre, add almost all the water and mix with a flat-bladed knife, using a cutting action, until the mixture comes together in beads, adding the remaining water if needed. Gently gather the dough together and lift out onto a lightly floured surface.

2 Roll the dough out between two sheets of baking paper to line the base and side of a lightly greased 22 cm (8 in) loose-bottomed flan tin. Ease the pastry into the tin and trim the edge, then chill for 15 minutes. Preheat the oven to 200°C (400°F/ Gas 6) and heat a baking tray.

3 Line the pastry with a sheet of baking paper and pour in some baking beads or rice, then bake on the heated baking tray for 15 minutes. Remove the paper and beads and bake for 10–15 minutes, or until dry and golden. Cool completely.

4 Meanwhile, put the strawberries, vanilla, Drambuie and 1 tablespoon of the brown sugar in a bowl and mix well. Put the mascarpone cheese, cream, zest and remaining brown sugar in another bowl and mix. Cover both bowls and refrigerate for 30 minutes, tossing the strawberries once or twice.

5 Whip half the mascarpone cream until firm, then evenly spoon it into the tart shell. Drain the strawberries, reserving the liquid. Pile the strawberries onto the tart. Serve wedges of the tart with a drizzling of the reserved liquid and a dollop of the remaining mascarpone cream.

UPSIDE-DOWN BANANA CAKE

SERVES 8

It's easy to bake a good banana cake as the fruit makes it so fabulously moist. Use this recipe to boost your confidence if you're not too sure of your baking abilities.

Preparation time: 20 minutes
Total cooking time: 45 minutes

50 g (1 3/4 oz) unsalted butter, melted
60 g (1/3 cup) soft brown sugar
6 large ripe bananas
125 g (4 1/2 oz) softened butter
230 g (1 1/4 cups) soft brown sugar,
    extra
2 eggs, lightly beaten
185 g (1 1/2 cups) self-raising flour
1 teaspoon baking powder

1 Preheat the oven to 180°C (350°F/Gas 4). Grease and line a 20 cm (8 in) square cake tin, pour the melted butter over the base of the tin and sprinkle with the brown sugar. Arrange 4 of the bananas, halved lengthways, cut-side-down, over the sugar.

2 Cream the butter and extra soft brown sugar until a light and fluffy mixture forms. Gradually add the eggs, beating well after each addition.

3 Sift the flour and baking powder into a bowl, then fold into the cake mixture with 2 mashed bananas. Carefully spread into the cake tin. Bake for 45 minutes, or until golden brown and a skewer comes out clean when inserted in the centre of the cake. Turn out while still warm. Serve the cake, banana-side-up, with cream or vanilla ice cream, if desired.

POACHED PEARS IN SAFFRON CITRUS SYRUP

SERVES 4

Saffron comes from the dried stigmas of autumn crocus flowers. Most recipes only call for a small amount of saffron threads—it is a costly spice because the stigmas are individually gathered by hand.

Preparation time: 10 minutes
Total cooking time: 30 minutes

1 vanilla bean, split lengthways
1/2 teaspoon saffron threads
185 g (3/4 cup) caster (superfine)
    sugar
2 teaspoons grated lemon zest
4 pears, peeled
whipped cream, to serve (optional)
biscotti, to serve (optional)

1 Put the vanilla bean, saffron threads, sugar, lemon zest and 500 ml (2 cups) of water in a large saucepan and mix together well. Heat, stirring, over a low heat until the sugar has dissolved. Bring to the boil, then reduce to a gentle simmer.

2 Add the pears and cook, covered, for 12–15 minutes, or until tender when tested with a metal skewer. Turn the pears over with a slotted spoon halfway through cooking. Once cooked, remove from the syrup with a slotted spoon.

3 Remove the lid and allow the saffron citrus syrup to come to the boil. Cook for 8–10 minutes, or until the syrup has reduced by half and thickened slightly. Remove the vanilla bean and drizzle the syrup over the pears. Serve with whipped cream and a couple of pieces of biscotti.

MANGO PANNA COTTA

SERVES 4

Mangoes are a universal favourite used in many different ways. Asian cuisines serve them green in salads, and they make a great sweet or hot pickle. Here they are given an Italian twist.

Preparation time: 30 minutes + 4 hours refrigeration
Total cooking time: 10 minutes

2 mangoes
2 teaspoons lime juice
3½ sheets gelatine
1 vanilla bean
500 ml (2 cups) cream
80 ml (⅓ cup) milk
125 g (½ cup) caster (superfine)
   sugar
1 teaspoon finely chopped mint

1 Peel 1 mango, then roughly chop the flesh and place it in a food processor with the lime juice and process until smooth. Push the purée through a fine strainer into a bowl.

2 Soak the gelatine leaves in cold water for about 10 minutes.

3 Meanwhile, cut the vanilla bean in half lengthways, then scrape out the seeds. Put the vanilla seeds and pod, cream, milk and sugar in a saucepan and stir to dissolve the sugar, then simmer over a medium heat, stirring occasionally, for 10 minutes. Remove from the heat and leave to infuse for 5 minutes, then strain into a clean bowl.

4 Remove the gelatine sheets from the water and squeeze out any excess moisture. Add the sheets to the cream mixture and stir until the gelatine has dissolved. Pour in the mango purée and mix together.

5 Pour the mixture into four lightly oiled 185 ml (¾ cup) moulds, cover with plastic wrap and refrigerate for 4 hours, or until set. Meanwhile, cube the remaining mango, sprinkle with the mint, then cover and refrigerate until ready to serve.

6 To serve, quickly dip the moulds into a bowl of warm water, then loosen the panna cotta with a knife if necessary before carefully tipping out onto a plate. Serve topped with the mango and mint.

WHITE CHOCOLATE AND
RASPBERRY CHEESECAKE

SERVES 8

From its biscuity base to its chocolate and cheese centre, this is a rich and creamy dessert for those who like to satisfy their sweet tooth ... and let's face it, who doesn't?

Preparation time: 40 minutes + cooling time
Total cooking time: 1 hour

375 g (13 oz) digestive biscuits,
   finely crushed
185 g (6½ oz) unsalted butter,
   melted
500 g (2 cups) cream cheese,
   at room temperature
90 g (⅓ cup) caster (superfine)
   sugar
4 eggs, lightly beaten
300 g (10½ oz) sour cream
320 g (11 oz) white chocolate
   buttons, melted and cooled
225 g (8 oz) raspberries

RASPBERRY SAUCE
300 g (10½ oz) fresh or frozen
   raspberries
1 tablespoon icing sugar

1 Grease a 23 cm (9 in) round springform cake tin and line the base and side with baking paper. Put the biscuits and butter in a bowl and mix together. Press the mixture firmly into the base and side of the tin and refrigerate for 10 minutes. Preheat the oven to 160°C (315°F/Gas 2–3).

2 Beat the cream cheese and sugar together until smooth and creamy. Add the eggs gradually, beating well after each addition. Beat in the sour cream and 250 g (9 oz) of the cooled white chocolate buttons. Pour half the mixture into the chilled base and sprinkle with the berries, reserving a few for a garnish. Top with the remaining cream cheese mixture, then place on a baking tray and bake for 50–60 minutes, or until set. Cool to room temperature.

3 Meanwhile, place the remaining melted chocolate in a piping bag with a thin plain nozzle. Pipe decorative shapes onto baking paper. Set.

4 To make the raspberry sauce, put the raspberries and icing sugar in a food processor and process until smooth. Strain through a fine sieve.

5 Serve wedges of the cheesecake with a drizzle of sauce, some berries and decorated with chocolate shapes.

BERRY AND RICOTTA
CREAM TARTLETS

SERVES 6

Ricotta that's cut from a wheel will be much firmer in texture than any other form. If you buy it in a tub, allow it to drain by wrapping it in muslin then putting it in a sieve over a bowl and leaving it overnight.

Preparation time: 1 hour + 1 hours refrigeration + 10 minutes resting
Total cooking time: 40 minutes

PASTRY
185 g (1½ cups) plain (all-purpose)
    flour
95 g (½ cup) ground almonds
40 g (⅓ cup) icing (confectioners')
    sugar
125 g (4½ oz) unsalted butter,
    chopped
1 egg, lightly beaten

FILLING
200 g (7 oz) ricotta cheese
1 teaspoon vanilla essence
2 eggs
160 g (⅔ cup) caster (superfine)
    sugar
125 ml (½ cup) cream
60 g (½ cup) raspberries
80 g (½ cup) blueberries
icing (confectioners') sugar, to dust

1 Sift the flour into a large bowl, then add the almonds and icing sugar. Rub the butter into the flour with your fingertips until it resembles fine breadcrumbs. Make a well in the centre and add the egg and mix with a flat-bladed knife, using a cutting action, until the mixture comes together in beads. Gently gather the dough together and lift out onto a lightly floured work surface. Press together into a ball, cover with plastic wrap and refrigerate for 30 minutes.

2 Grease six 8 cm (3 in) loose-bottomed tart tins. Divide the pastry into six and roll each piece out between two sheets of baking paper to fit the base and side of the tins. Ease the pastry into the tins, gently press into shape and trim the edges. Prick the bases with a fork, then refrigerate for 30 minutes. Preheat the oven to 180°C (350°F/Gas 4).

3 Line the pastry with a sheet of crumpled baking paper and spread with a layer of baking beads or uncooked rice. Bake for 8–10 minutes. Remove the paper and beads from the pastry case.

4 Meanwhile, process the ricotta cheese, vanilla, eggs, sugar and cream in a food processor until smooth.

5 Divide the berries and filling among the tarts and bake for 25–30 minutes, or until the filling is just set—the top should be soft but not too wobbly. Cool. Dust with icing sugar and serve.

ORANGE AND ALMOND CAKE

SERVES 6–8

The use of ground almonds rather than flour makes this a rich, heavy cake, which is delicious served with cream. You'll also find the syrup soaks into the cake, making it wonderfully moist.

Preparation time: 25 minutes
Total cooking time: 3 hours

5 large oranges
6 eggs, separated
1 tablespoon orange flower water
    or orange liqueur
250 g (1 cup) caster (superfine)
    sugar
300 g (10½ oz) ground almonds
1 teaspoon baking powder
cream, to serve (optional)

ORANGE SYRUP
500 ml (2 cups) fresh orange juice,
    strained
185 g (3/4 cup) caster (superfine)
    sugar
60 ml (1/4 cup) Sauternes

1 Grease and lightly flour a 23 cm (9 in) springform cake tin, tipping out any excess flour.

2 Wipe 2 of the oranges with a damp cloth to remove any dirt. Put the whole oranges into a medium saucepan full of water and boil for 2 hours, topping up with water as it evaporates. Remove the oranges.

3 Preheat the oven to 180°C (350°F/Gas 4). Cut the oranges into quarters and place in a food processor. Process until smooth, then cool thoroughly.

4 Put the egg yolks, orange flower water and caster sugar in a large bowl and beat until smooth, then stir in the orange purée and mix well. Whisk the egg whites in a clean, dry bowl until firm peaks form.

5 Add the ground almonds and baking powder to the orange mixture, stir together well, then carefully fold in the egg whites. Gently pour into the prepared cake tin and place on the middle shelf of the oven for 1 hour, or until firm to touch. Cover the cake with foil if it is browning too quickly. Cool the cake in the tin before transferring it to a serving plate.

6 Meanwhile, to make the syrup, place the orange juice, sugar and Sauternes in a saucepan over a medium heat and stir until the sugar is dissolved. Reduce the heat and simmer for about 20 minutes, or until reduced by half and slightly syrupy, skimming off any scum that forms on the surface. The syrup will thicken as it cools.

7 Peel the remaining 3 oranges and remove all pith and sinew. Cut each orange into thin slices. Cut the cake into wedges and top with orange slices and drizzle with the syrup. Serve with cream.

COFFEE MERINGUE ROLL

This recipe calls for a soft meringue, as it's easier to roll up than a crisp dry case. Don't overcook it—the centre should still be sweet and sticky.

Preparation time: 30 minutes + cooling time
Total cooking time: 30 minutes

MERINGUE
4 egg whites, at room temperature
185 g (3/4 cup) caster (superfine)
    sugar
1 teaspoon vanilla essence
2 teaspoons white vinegar
2 teaspoons cornflour
30 g (1/3 cup) flaked almonds

TOFFEE PRALINE
30 g (1/3 cup) flaked almonds
340 g (1 1/3 cups) caster (superfine)
    sugar

COFFEE CREAM
125 ml (1/2 cup) cream
4–5 tablespoons very strong cold
    black coffee
2 tablespoons icing (confectioners')
    sugar
250 g (9 oz) mascarpone cheese

1 Preheat the oven to 160°C (315°F/Gas 2–3). Lightly grease a 30 x 25 cm (12 x 10 in) swiss roll tin and line the base and sides with baking paper. To make the meringue, beat the egg whites in a dry bowl until firm peaks form. Gradually beat in the sugar, beating for 5–8 minutes, or until the sugar has dissolved and the mixture is thick and glossy. Fold in the vanilla, vinegar and cornflour, then spread into the prepared tin and smooth the top. Sprinkle with almonds, then bake for 20 minutes, or until firm.

2 Meanwhile, to make the toffee praline, cover a baking tray with baking paper and sprinkle with almonds. Put the sugar and 125 ml (1/2 cup) water in a small saucepan and stir over a low heat until the sugar dissolves. Bring to the boil and simmer without stirring until the toffee is dark golden —watch carefully as it can burn quickly. Pour over the almonds and leave until set. Break into small pieces or pulverise in a food processor. Set aside.

3 Put a large sheet of baking paper on a work surface and sprinkle with a tablespoon of caster sugar. Invert the meringue onto the paper so that the almonds are on the bottom. Peel off the paper and leave for 10 minutes.

4 To make the coffee cream, beat the cream in a small bowl until firm peaks form. Gently stir in the coffee, icing sugar and mascarpone and mix. Do not overbeat or it will curdle. Spread the meringue with the coffee cream and roll up firmly. Transfer to a plate. Sprinkle the toffee praline down the centre of the log, slice and serve.

INDEX

Published by Murdoch Books® a division of Murdoch Magazines Pty Ltd,
GPO Box 1203, Sydney NSW Australia 1045

Editorial Director: Diana Hill. Editors: Lucy Campbell, Zoë Harpham, Stephanie Kistner.
Creative Director: Marylouise Brammer. Concept Designer: Michelle Cutler. Designer: Annette Fitzgerald.
Photographers: Joe Filshie, Ian Hofstetter, Rob Reichenfeld. Stylists: Marie-Hélène Clauzon, Georgina Dolling,
Cherise Koch, Michelle Noerianto. Food Directors: Lulu Grimes, Jane Lawson. Food Editors: Vanessa Broadfoot,
Kathleen Gandy, Melita Smilovic. Recipe Development: Ruth Armstrong, Fiona Hammond, Eva Katz, Jane Lawson,
Michelle Lawton, Barbara Lowery, Kerrie Mullins, Kate Murdoch, Maria Papadopoulos, Wendy Quisumbing, Jody
Vassallo. Home Economists: Valli Little, Ben Masters, Briget Palmer, Wendy Quisumbing. Food Preparation: Justine
Johnson, Valli Little, Kate Murdoch, Angela Tregonning.

Chief Executive: Juliet Rogers
Publisher: Kay Scarlett
Production Manager: Kylie Kirkwood

National Library of Australia Cataloguing-in-Publication data
Indulgence. Includes index. ISBN 1 74045 188 0.
1. Cookery. 2. Cookery, International. 3. Dinners and dining.
641.5

Printed by Toppan Printing Hong Kong Co. Ltd.
PRINTED IN CHINA

Indulgence has been compiled from recipes in the Murdoch Books publications *Modern Australian Food*,
Entertaining: Quick Short Recipes and *Quick and Easy Workday Dinners*
Copyright ©Text, design, photography and illustrations Murdoch Books® 2002.
All rights reserved. No part of this publication may be reproduced, stored in a retrieval system
or transmitted in any form or by any means, electronic, mechanical, photocopying, recording
or otherwise without the prior written permission of the publisher.
Murdoch Books® is a trademark of Murdoch Magazines Pty Ltd.

The publisher thanks the following for assistance: MUD Australia; Chef Australia; Breville Holdings Pty Ltd; Kambrook,
Sheldon & Hammond; Bertolli Olive Oil; Southcorp Appliances.